# Bible Study Guide

## Revelation

### Good Questions Have
### Small Groups Talking

## By Josh Hunt

# Contents

Revelation, Lesson #1 . . . . . . . . . . . . . . . . . . . 1

Revelation, Lesson #2 . . . . . . . . . . . . . . . . . 20

Revelation, Lesson #3 . . . . . . . . . . . . . . . . 37

Revelation, Lesson #4 . . . . . . . . . . . . . . . . 56

Revelation, Lesson #5 . . . . . . . . . . . . . . . . 76

Revelation, Lesson #6 . . . . . . . . . . . . . . . . 92

Revelation, Lesson #7 . . . . . . . . . . . . . . . 110

# Revelation, Lesson #1
## Good Questions Have Small Groups Talking
### www.joshhunt.com

My dad recommended to me that if you want to understand Revelation, read Revelation. Get familiar with the book itself. You might challenge your people to read through the book of Revelation each week as we go through this study. Encourage them to get a Study Bible and read the notes. Imagine a group where everyone read the text and a different Study Bible so we could all share insights into what we read. If you would like to buy a commentary, I recommend Craig S. Keener, *Revelation, The NIV Application Commentary* (Grand Rapids, MI: Zondervan Publishing House, 1999)

## Revelation 1

## OPEN
Let's each share your name and one thing you are grateful for.

## DIG
1. **Introduction / overview. What do you know about this book? What do we have to look forward to?**

   Just as Genesis is the book of beginnings, so Revelation is the book of completion. In it, we see how God finalizes the divine program of redemption and vindicates His holy name before all creation.

Although the Gospels and Epistles contain numerous prophecies, only Revelation among all the New Testament books focuses primarily on prophetic events. It borrows heavily from Old Testament symbols and passages, and seems to have a special connection to the Book of Daniel. Because of this potent imagery, it is often difficult to know in Revelation when the author is speaking literally and when he is speaking symbolically.

Revelation also features several high moments of worship in which the residents of heaven and the saints of God praise the Lord for His holy character and righteous judgments. These extraordinary times of worship are usually presented as joyful songs of praise (see Rev. 4:8–11; 5:8–14; 7:9–12; 11:15–18; 15:2–4; 16:5–7; 19:1–7).

The title of this book in the Greek text is Apokalypsis Ioannou, "Revelation of John." It is also known as the Apocalypse, a transliteration of the word apokalypsis, meaning "unveiling," "disclosure," or "revelation." Thus the book unveils what otherwise could not be known. A better title comes from the first verse, the "Revelation of Jesus Christ." This could be taken as a revelation that came from Christ, or as a revelation about Christ; both are appropriate.

Revelation was originally written to seven local churches in Asia Minor (modern Turkey), but its message applies to all Christians everywhere. Jesus is coming again in great power and glory, and His certain return should motivate us every day to Spirit-filled, loving action on His behalf. — Charles F. Stanley, *The Charles F. Stanley Life Principles Bible: New King James Version* (Nashville, TN: Nelson Bibles, 2005), Re.

## 2. What does Revelation mean?

The word translated "revelation" simply means "unveiling." It gives us our English word apocalypse which, unfortunately, is today a synonym for chaos and catastrophe. The verb simply means "to uncover, to reveal, to make manifest." In this book, the Holy Spirit pulls back the curtain and gives us the privilege of seeing the glorified Christ in heaven and the fulfillment of His sovereign purposes in the world.

In other words, Revelation is an open book in which God reveals His plans and purposes to His church. When Daniel finished writing his prophecy, he was instructed to "shut up the words, and seal the book" (Dan. 12:4); but John was given opposite instructions: "Seal not the sayings of the prophecy of this book" (Rev. 22:10). Why? Since Calvary, the Resurrection, and the coming of the Holy Spirit, God has ushered in the "last days" (Heb. 1:1-2) and is fulfilling His hidden purposes in this world. "The time is at hand" (Rev. 1:3; 22:10).

John's prophecy is primarily the revelation of Jesus Christ, not the revelation of future events. You must not divorce the Person from the prophecy, for without the Person there could be no fulfillment of the prophecy. "He is not incidental to its action," wrote Dr. Merrill Tenney. "He is its chief Subject." In Revelation 1-3, Christ is seen as the exalted Priest-King ministering to the churches. In Revelation 4-5, He is seen in heaven as the glorified Lamb of God, reigning on the throne. In Revelation 6-18, Christ is the Judge of all the earth; and in Revelation 19, He returns to earth as the conquering King of kings. The book closes with the heavenly Bridegroom ushering His bride, the church, into the glorious heavenly city.

Whatever you do as you study this book, get to know your Saviour better. — *The Bible Exposition Commentary – New Testament, Volume 2.*

3. **What is the big idea—the main point—of the book of Revelation?**

ALTHOUGH MANY DETAILS in Revelation (and in this commentary) are debatable, the basic thrust is not. The true and living God summons us from our preoccupation with the world to recognize, in light of his ultimate plan for history, what really matters and what really does not. God first gave Revelation to a culture where people would hear the words of the book and imagine the stark and terrifying images; to be struck by the full force of the book, we must likewise use our imaginations to grasp the images of terror. Revelation is not meant for casual or "lite" reading; to genuinely hear it summons us to grapple with God's judgment on a world in rebellion against him. — Craig S. Keener, *Revelation, The NIV Application Commentary* (Grand Rapids, MI: Zondervan Publishing House, 1999), 21.

4. **Which do you think is more important in understanding of this book—and understanding of the world in which it is written, or an understanding of current events?**

SOME READERS BELIEVE that current events unlock the meaning of the biblical prophecies. Thus, for example, one writer opines that even Luther and Calvin "knew little about prophecy," but that study-Bible editor C. I. Scofield rightly pointed out that Revelation was written to allow end-time interpreters to unlock its meaning.

Yet this approach seems to me wrongheaded—I believe that it runs up against the evidence of Revelation itself. John writes to seven literal churches in literal Asia Minor, following the same sequence in which a messenger traveling Roman roads would deliver the book (see the more detailed comment in the Bridging Contexts section on 1:4–8). If we take seriously what the book itself claims, then it was a book that must have made good sense to its first hearers, who in fact were "blessed" for obeying it (1:3). That John wrote the book in Greek probably suggests that he also used figures of speech and symbols that were part of his culture more than ours. That the book was to remain "unsealed" even in his generation also indicates that it was meant to be understood from that time forward (22:10; contrast Dan. 12:9–10).

Perhaps an even more compelling reason exists to argue for focusing on ancient rather than modern background for understanding the book of Revelation. If today's newspapers are a necessary key to interpreting the book, then no generation until our own could have understood and obeyed the book (contrary to the assumption in 1:3). They could not have read the book as Scripture profitable for teaching and correction—an approach that does not fit a high view of biblical authority (cf. 2 Tim. 3:16–17). If, however, the book was understandable for the first generation, subsequent generations can profit from the book simply by learning some history. Some popular prophecy teachers have ignored much of the history that is available, preferring to interpret the book in light of current newspaper headings. That is probably why most of them have to revise their predictions every few years as the headlines change.

Another matter of interpretation is that some want to take everything in Revelation literally. Whether one should attempt this approach depends in a sense on what one means by the term literally. When Reformers like Luther talked about interpreting the Bible "literally," they were using a technical designation (sensus literalis) that meant taking each part of Scripture according to its "literary sense," hence including attention to genre or literary type. But they did not mean that we should downplay figures of speech or symbols. We should take literally historical narrative in the Bible, but Revelation belongs to a different genre, a mixture of prophetic and "apocalyptic" genres, both of which are full of symbols. The Reformers did not demand that we interpret symbols as if they were not symbols, and this kind of literalism is actually at odds with what they meant.

In fact, to take every symbol in Revelation nonsymbolically is so difficult that no one ever really attempts it. No one takes Babylon the Great as a literal prostitute or mother of prostitutes (17:5), no one takes new Jerusalem as a literal individual who is a bride, and few Protestants take the mother in chapter 12 as a literal mother (certainly not one literally clothed with the sun). "Take literally as much as possible," comes the response. But the amount that is "possible" is usually determined by one's presuppositions. Are literal monsters like those in chapter 9 possible? God could certainly create them, but they do bear many striking resemblances to creatures that simply represent locusts in the book of Joel. Is it not more important to be consistent with how the rest of Revelation and prophetic literature invites us to interpret them (much of which is plainly symbolic) than to try to take all its language literally? Is it not more respectful to Revelation to hear it on its own terms (symbols included) than to read into it a system of interpretation the book itself nowhere claims? That Revelation clearly includes symbols and sometimes tells us what they mean (e.g., 1:20) should lead us to suspect any interpretive method that ignores the intense symbolism of the rest of the book. — Craig S. Keener, *Revelation, The NIV Application Commentary* (Grand Rapids, MI: Zondervan Publishing House, 1999), 21–23.

## 5. What bad things come from misinterpreting Revelation?

THE MASSIVE LOSS of life among David Koresh's followers in Waco, Texas, involved a misreading of the book of Revelation. Prophetic speculation is not, however, a new phenomenon. Jewish works sometimes guessed numbers and times still future—and history proved them wrong (e.g., Sib. Or. 11.265–67; Test. Moses 2:3). Early church fathers also indulged in some speculations that never materialized, such as Hippolytus's view that the world would end in A.D. 500. Unfortunately, many modern prophecy teachers have not scored much better.

Jerome studied in biblical lands to better understand the literary forms and contexts of the Bible, including Revelation. Many interpreters, however, have failed to learn the original setting of the book and have in effect "added to" it, despite its warning (22:18), by reading into it theological systems not justified by the text itself. Of course, Jehovah's Witnesses are known for such activities. Whereas most groups that have set dates gave up after they missed once or twice, "Jehovah's Witnesses won't quit. Their leaders have earmarked the years 1874, 1878, 1881, 1910, 1914, 1918, 1925, 1975, and 1984 as times of eschatological significance."7 Religion scholars have noted how various sects like Mormons, Jehovah's Witnesses, and Christian Science adherents have used Revelation arbitrarily to support the views they already held. Because Jehovah's Witnesses are the best-known purveyors of prophetic pessimism that never panned out, and also because readers of this commentary will be fairly unanimous that the Witnesses are in error, I often use them in this commentary to illustrate obvious errors in interpretive method.

But unfortunately, while Jehovah's Witnesses are the best-known transgressors, history is littered with such failed predictions from all segments of Christendom, perhaps most obviously in the twentieth century from popular evangelicalism. In the 1920s, some dispensational prophecy teachers viewed The Protocols of the Elders of Zion—now recognized as a forgery promoted by the Nazis—as confirming their prophetic ideas. (Some later repudiated the Protocols, but others never did.) To their credit, this stream of prophetic interpretation proved strikingly right about Israel's becoming a nation, a significant matter (although it is also true that they were not the only group to expect it).10 The parts of the body of Christ involved in this stream of interpretation also often demonstrated a commendable commitment to missions and world evangelism second to none. But when speculating on details, many popular prognosticators proved wrong on the identity of the Antichrist and other matters. "Nobody anticipated the demise of the Soviet empire or most aspects of the Gulf War. When history takes unexpected turns, the experts have to make adjustments, redraw their maps, and come out with new editions."

Lest we think that evangelicals on the whole learned humility from early mistakes, plenty of examples provide warnings to the contrary. In 1979 Colin Deal's book showing why Christ would return by 1988 circulated information about a computer in Belgium known as "the beast," claiming that this was the Antichrist. His source seemed "unaware that the computer was only a fictional creation from a novel."13 That the devil could lure modern interpreters into such errors is not surprising; Saint Martin of Tours, who died in 397, alleged that "there is no doubt that the Antichrist has already been born." (If Martin is right, the Antichrist displays remarkable longevity.) Others predicted his coming for the years 1000, 1184, 1186, 1229, 1345, 1385, etc. — Craig S.

Keener, *Revelation, The NIV Application Commentary* (Grand Rapids, MI: Zondervan Publishing House, 1999), 23–25.

## 6. Who could summarize the major views on Revelation?

Every end-time view can seem reasonable if one has never sympathetically studied other views. Thus I wish that all those committed to particular end-time scenarios would survey Richard Kyle's The Last Days Are Here Again (Grand Rapids: Baker, 1998), Dwight Wilson's Armageddon Now! The Premillenarian Response to Russia and Israel Since 1917 (Grand Rapids: Baker, 1977), Gary DeMar's Last Days Madness: The Folly of Trying to Predict When Christ Will Return (Brentwood, Tenn.: Wolgemuth & Hyatt, 1991), or other works like these. By reviewing the history of end-times speculation littered with failed predictions and even the varied views on major end-times issues by respected Christian leaders, they help us put our own views in perspective.

One may take as an example of diverse end-time views among Christians the Millennium, or the thousand-year reign of Christ in Revelation 20. Does Jesus return before the future Millennium (the premillennial view, the most common among North American evangelicals today) or after it (the postmillennial view), or is this period merely a symbol for the present era (the amillennial view)? Many readers may be surprised to learn that most Christian leaders in history were amillennial (like Augustine, Luther, and Calvin), many leaders in North American revivals were postmillennial (like Jonathan Edwards and Charles Finney), and most of the early church fathers were premillennial (but posttribulational).

If Calvin, Wesley, Finney, Moody, and most Christians today each have held different views, is it possible that God's blessing may not rest solely on those who hold a particular end-time view? If different views strongly dominated different eras of history (e.g., amillennialism during the Reformation; postmillennialism during the U.S. Great Awakenings; premillennialism today), is it possible that our own views are more historically shaped than we care to admit? Studying various views better equips us to read Revelation more objectively on its own terms. — Craig S. Keener, *Revelation, The NIV Application Commentary* (Grand Rapids, MI: Zondervan Publishing House, 1999), 25–26.

**7. We always want to read the Bible for application. What are some of the main application points we can look forward to in Revelation?**

What then is Revelation's message? We mention several points below, though we develop most of them later in the commentary on specific passages.

- That God is awesomely majestic, as well as sovereign in our troubles

- That Jesus' sacrifice as the Lamb ultimately brings complete deliverance for those who trust him

- That God's judgments on the world are often to serve notice on the world that God will avenge his people

- That regardless of how things appear in the short run, "sin does not go unpunished," and God will judge

- That God can accomplish his purposes through a small and persecuted remnant; he is not dependent on what the world values as power

- That worship leads us from grief over our sufferings to God's eternal purposes seen from a heavenly perspective

- That proclaiming Christ invites persecution, the normal state of committed believers in this age

- That Christ is worth dying for

- That a radical contrast exists between God's kingdom (exemplified in the bride, the new Jerusalem) and the world's values (exemplified in the prostitute, Babylon)

- That the hope God has prepared for us far exceeds our present sufferings

- That God's plan and church ultimately include representatives of all peoples

Craig S. Keener, *Revelation, The NIV Application Commentary* (Grand Rapids, MI: Zondervan Publishing House, 1999), 41–42.

## 8. Verse 1. When can we expect these events to take place?

What must soon take place must be understood from the perspective of heaven rather than earth. With God, a thousand years is only a day (2 Pet. 3:8). This means that the events described in Revelation were written down less than two days ago! If they do not come to pass for another two or three days, that will still be "soon." Jesus used a revealing angel to communicate part of the revelation to his servant John (for example, see Rev. 19:9), who describes himself, too, as a "slave" or "bondservant." — Kendell H. Easley, *Revelation, vol. 12, Holman New Testament Commentary* (Nashville, TN: Broadman & Holman Publishers, 1998), 12.

### 9. Verse 3. What does it mean to take this message to heart?

The initiative for the book is not found in earth, but in heaven. The risen Jesus granted John four spectacular visions that he was instructed to record and send to the persecuted Christians of Asia. John was certainly aware of the importance and authority of what he wrote. He promises divine blessing for faithful obedience to the book's teachings. These blessings apply to every generation of Jesus' followers who read and heed. This is the first of seven times blessed is proclaimed in the book (see also 14:13; 16:15; 19:9, 20:6; 22:7, 14). It means "how fortunate" or "oh, the joy of." Jesus used it repeatedly in the Sermon on the Mount (Matt. 5:3–10). Three activities are recommended: to read, to hear, and to take to heart. The setting implied is a local congregation. In a time of little literacy, one oral reader (he who reads) addressed many listeners (those who hear it). Both reader and hearers are to obey (take to heart what is written). This verb can also be translated "keep" or "observe." Jesus used the same verb in John 14–15 in reference to keeping the commands of the Father (for example, John 14:15; 15:10). The time is near because these events "must soon take place." — Kendell H. Easley, *Revelation, vol. 12, Holman New Testament Commentary* (Nashville, TN: Broadman & Holman Publishers, 1998), 13.

### 10. Verse 4. Who is this book addressed to? Can you locate these churches on a map?

The book is addressed to 'the seven churches that are in Asia'. These churches are mentioned in verse 11. They were located in the Roman proconsular province of Asia, that is, the western part of Asia Minor. The seven, beginning with Ephesus, which was nearest—and perhaps dearest—to John in Patmos, then proceeding north to Smyrna and

Pergamum, then south-east to Thyatira, Sardis, Philadelphia and Laodicea, formed a kind of irregular circle. It is helpful to consult a Bible map here. These seven churches represent the entire Church throughout this dispensation. — William Hendriksen, *More than Conquerors: An Interpretation of the Book of Revelation* (Grand Rapids, MI: Baker Books, 1967), 52.

## 11. Verse 4. Grace is a word we use in church a lot, but not so much outside of church. What exactly does it mean?

Grace is God's favour given to those who do not deserve it, pardoning their sins and bestowing upon them the gift of eternal life. — William Hendriksen, *More than Conquerors: An Interpretation of the Book of Revelation* (Grand Rapids, MI: Baker Books, 1967), 53.

## 12. Verse 4. What or who are the seven spirits?

The expression 'the seven spirits' refers to the Holy Spirit in the fullness of His operations and influences in the world and in the Church. — William Hendriksen, *More than Conquerors: An Interpretation of the Book of Revelation* (Grand Rapids, MI: Baker Books, 1967), 53.

## 13. Do you find a reference to the Trinity in this passage?

Peace, the reflection of the smile of God in the heart of the believer who has been reconciled to God through Jesus Christ, is the result of grace. This grace and this peace are provided by the Father, dispensed by the Holy Spirit, and merited for us by the Son. Therefore all three are mentioned in the salutation. Literally we read: 'Grace to you and peace from "He who is and was and is coming". This is both good Greek and good English. — William Hendriksen, *More than*

*Conquerors: An Interpretation of the Book of Revelation* (Grand Rapids, MI: Baker Books, 1967), 53.

## 14. What do we learn about Jesus from this section?

The reference to "the seven spirits who are before his throne" (1:4) is a reference to the Holy Spirit, and so by greeting the churches with grace and peace from the Father, the Spirit, and the Son, John has greeted them with grace from all three persons of the Godhead. Following this Trinitarian formula, John identifies Jesus in three ways in 1:5. He is, first, "the faithful witness." John has identified himself as one who "bore witness" (1:2, cf. 1:9), and other Christians in the book who are described as witnesses are, like Jesus, slain— Antipas in 2:13, the two witnesses in 11:3, 7, and those on whose blood the harlot was drunk in 17:6 (cf. 6:9; 12:11; 19:10; 20:4). Jesus is "the faithful witness," and his people follow him by faithfully bearing witness.

The second way in which Jesus is identified in 1:5 is as "the firstborn of the dead." This phrase points to the way that Jesus has pioneered the resurrection from the dead. He is the first whose resurrection is not merely resuscitation of bodily life. When Jesus rose, he rose in a glorified body. Revelation 20:4 indicates that those who are faithful unto death like he was will be raised from the dead like he was.

The third description of Jesus in 1:5 is that he is "the ruler of kings on earth." However powerful Domitian or any other ruler might be, they all answer to Jesus. He will call them to account. Jesus is the King. — James M. Hamilton Jr., *Preaching the Word: Revelation—The Spirit Speaks to the Churches*, ed. R. Kent Hughes (Wheaton, IL: Crossway, 2012), 35–36.

## 15. What do we learn about ourselves?

John addresses the doxology "To him who loves us" (1:5b). This is the first thing Jesus has done for his people. Notice that this statement is made in the present tense. Jesus loves his people. Jesus' love for his people led him to lay down his life, and what Jesus accomplished by laying down his life is identified in the final words of verse 5: "and has freed us from our sins by his blood." This is the second thing Jesus has done for his people. The blood of Jesus frees us from our sins in the sense that his death cancels our obligation to pay the penalty of our sins to the Father. Those who sin deserve to die. Death is separation from God. Jesus died that death so that his people could be reconciled to God and live. Jesus' death was a penal, substitutionary atonement. The word penal points to the fact that he paid the penalty. The word substitutionary means he died in place of his people as their substitute. The word atonement means that his death reconciled men to God.

Not only does his blood free us from the penalty of our sins, it also frees us from slavery to sin, which is elaborated upon in the next phrase. After stating at the end of verse 5 that Jesus "has freed us from our sins by his blood," John states the third thing Jesus has done for his people: "and made us a kingdom, priests to his God and Father" (1:6). The statement that he "made us a kingdom" points to the fact that we now belong to King Jesus. Our obligation is no longer to the prince of the power of the air, the ruler of this age, Satan. Jesus made us his kingdom. We are his people. The blood of Jesus frees people from lust, greed, pride, anger, and every other enslaving sin. The blood of Jesus breaks the power of canceled sin. The kingdom of Jesus cannot be overcome by any worldly power. — James M. Hamilton Jr., *Preaching the Word: Revelation—The Spirit Speaks to the Churches*, ed. R. Kent Hughes (Wheaton, IL: Crossway, 2012), 36.

## 16. What does it mean that we are priests? What is the application?

There is the idea of the priesthood. It was an offering made for man to God by the priest. The priest was to represent God to man and man to God. Before God, he pleads for the man he represents. He instructs. He exhorts. With complete sympathy and understanding, he goes to God for man. This he can do because he himself is a man.

But the breakdown in the Old Testament was that the priest, when he went before God, to stand between a holy God and fallen man, was embarrassed, because he had to atone not only for the sins of the people he was reconciling, but he had to atone for his own sins as well. This was where the breakdown was. This was why Isaac Watts could write in his hymn "Not All the Blood of Beasts":

> Not all the blood of beasts
> On Jewish altars slain
> Could give the guilty conscience peace
> Or wash away the stain.
>
> But Christ, the heavenly Lamb,
> Takes all our sins away;
> A sacrifice of nobler name
> And richer blood than they.

The priest could not, by the blood of the sacrifice he made, take sin away completely, but only partly. God forgave sin and covered it until the time when Christ, the Great High Priest, came. When Christ came, He qualified completely as the one who could reconcile God and man. He was ordained of God. That was qualification number one. "Thou art my son. Thou art a priest forever." He wanted reconciliation for the people. He had compassion. Christ qualified as the priest, and He became the author, the source and the giver of eternal salvation. — A. W. Tozer, *Experiencing the Presence of God: Teachings from the Book of Hebrews*, ed. James L. Snyder (Ventura, CA: Regal, 2010), 60–61.

## 17. What do we learn about the second coming from this passage?

The New Testament repeatedly announces that Jesus Christ will one day return. His second "coming" or "presence" (Greek parousia) will be a royal visit. Christ's return will be personal and physical (Matt. 24:44; Acts 1:11; Col. 3:4; 2 Tim. 4:8; Heb. 9:28), visible and triumphant (Mark 8:38; 2 Thess. 1:10; Rev. 1:7)

At the Second Coming, Jesus will bring an end to history. He will raise the dead and judge the world (John 5:28, 29), and impart to God's children their final glory (Rom. 8:17, 18; Col. 3:4). Paul says that Christ will then deliver the kingdom and become subject to the Father (1 Cor. 15:24–28 note). In saying this, Paul does not mean that Christ is reduced in honor, but that He will have completed the plan God assigned to Him for redeeming the elect. In heaven, the elect will honor the Lamb who opened the book of God's salvation (Rev. 5).

According to 1 Thess. 4:16, 17, Christ's coming will be a descent from the sky, heralded by a trumpet, a shout, and the voice of the archangel. Those who have died in Christ will be raised, and Christians living on earth will be caught up to meet Christ. This event will mark the end of life in this world as we have known it, and the beginning of life in unbroken communion with God. The idea that Christians will be taken out of this world for a period after which Christ will appear still a third time for the "Second Coming" has been widely held, but lacks scriptural support. — R. C. Sproul, ed., *The Reformation Study Bible: English Standard*

*Version* (Orlando, FL; Lake Mary, FL: Ligonier Ministries, 2005), 1741.

## 18. Again, what is the application? What difference does the second coming make?

Christ teaches that it will be a tragic disaster for anyone who is not ready when He returns (Matt. 24:36–51). The thought of His return should be constantly in our minds, encouraging us in our present Christian service (1 Cor. 15:58) and teaching us to live ready to meet Christ at any time (Matt. 25:1–13). — R. C. Sproul, ed., *The Reformation Study Bible: English Standard Version* (Orlando, FL; Lake Mary, FL: Ligonier Ministries, 2005), 1741.

## 19. What do we learn about God from verse 8? Again, what is the application?

I AM YOURS FOR ALL ETERNITY. I am the Alpha and the Omega: the One who is and was and is to come. The world you inhabit is a place of constant changes—more than your mind can absorb without going into shock. Even the body you inhabit is changing relentlessly, in spite of modern science's attempts to prolong youth and life indefinitely. I, however, am the same yesterday and today and forever.

Because I never change, your relationship with Me provides a rock-solid foundation for your life. I will never leave your side. When you move on from this life to the next, My Presence beside you will shine brighter with each step. You have nothing to fear, because I am with you for all time and throughout eternity. — Sarah Young, *40 Days with Jesus: Celebrating His Presence* (Nashville: Thomas Nelson, 2011).

20. What do you want to recall from today's introduction to Revelation?

21. Who will join me in reading through the book of Revelation each week during this study?

22. How can we support one another in prayer this week?

My dad recommended to me that if you want to understand Revelation, read Revelation. Get familiar with the book itself. You might challenge your people to read through the book of Revelation each week as we go through this study. Encourage them to get a Study Bible and read the notes. Imagine a group where everyone read the text and a different Study Bible so we could all share insights into what we read. If you would like to buy a commentary, I recommend Craig S. Keener, *Revelation, The NIV Application Commentary* (Grand Rapids, MI: Zondervan Publishing House, 1999)

## Revelation 2, 3

## OPEN

Let's each share your name and when was the last time you wrote a letter?

## DIG

1. **Background / setting. What is life like for the church as John writes?**

   Although there has never been unanimity concerning the date of Revelation, the majority of evangelical scholarship follows the affirmation of Irenaeus that the time and occasion for the writing was the latter portion of Domitian's reign (A.D. 90–96). Characteristic of Domitian's assault on the embryonic Christian community was the practice of exile. John writes this epistle from exile on Patmos, a roughly horseshoe-shaped rock-quarry island about 6 miles wide and 10 miles long, approximately 25 miles off the coast of Asia Minor due west of Miletus. Patmos provided an ideal place of confinement for political prisoners. John possibly labored in the rock quarries alongside the rogues and slaves of the empire, chipping out the materials for pagan temples and state edifices. In the midst of such agonies, the Lord was uniquely revealed to John in a vision (cf. 1:1, 10–12). — W. A. Criswell et al., eds., *Believer's Study Bible, electronic ed*. (Nashville: Thomas Nelson, 1991), Re 1:1.

## 2. What do you know about Ephesus? Locate Ephesus on a map.

Ephesus was wealthy, prosperous, magnificent, and famous for its shrine of Diana. The city was located near the western coast of Asia Minor, on the Aegean Sea and near the mouth of the Cayster River. Its harbour—in the days of its glory—accommodated the largest ships. Moreover, it was easily accessible by land, for Ephesus was connected by highways with the most important cities of Asia Minor. Ephesus was for a long time the commercial centre of Asia. The temple of Diana was at the same time a treasure house, a museum, and a place of refuge for criminals. It furnished employment for many, including the silversmiths who made miniature shrines of Diana. — William Hendriksen, *More than Conquerors: An Interpretation of the Book of Revelation* (Grand Rapids, MI: Baker Books, 1967), 60.

## 3. What was the problem with the Ephesian church?

The corrective exhortation concerns the fact that, although they labored faithfully and showed discernment theologically, they had left their first love.

Notice He doesn't say they lost their first love. He says they left it.…

> While chopping trees for the expansion of their facility, the axe head of one of Elisha's students flew into the Jordan River. Ever feel like the cutting edge is gone from your ministry, like the power is absent from your life? Since wood is biblically symbolic of the flesh, this guy with the wooden handle still in his grasp could have said, I can still make noise banging trees with the handle. Maybe no one will notice that nothing's happening in the way of effective ministry." But he didn't. Instead, he did what Jesus tells you and me and those at Ephesus to do: he cried, "Master, it's not there anymore. The cutting edge is gone."

> "Take me to the place you had it last," said Elisha. And the young man took Elisha to the edge of the river where he had last seen the axe head. Elisha ripped off a limb from a nearby tree, put it in the river, and miraculously, the axe head floated to the top.

> "There it is, son," said Elisha. "Now reach in and grab it" (see 2 Kings 6:1–7).

It's a perfect picture of what Jesus is about to say to those at Ephesus and to those of us who have left our first love.…
— Jon Courson, *Jon Courson's Application Commentary* (Nashville, TN: Thomas Nelson, 2003), 1671.

## 4. What is meant by "first love"?

What is the "first love" that Jesus was speaking of in Revelation 2? It's similar to the kind of love that two newlyweds experience. This is mentioned in Jeremiah 2, where God says, " 'I remember you, the kindness of your youth, the love of your betrothal, when you went after Me in the wilderness, in a land not sown'" (verse 2). God was saying to Israel, "I remember when we had that honeymoon type of relationship." It was a close, intimate love.

This is not to say that two married people can and should have that feeling of butterflies in their stomachs forever. I remember that when I first met my wife, I would experience a loss of appetite and would get sort of jittery around her. Today, I am more in love with her than I have ever been, but I am not necessarily feeling those emotions that I felt when we first met.

In the same way, God is not saying that He expects us to walk around with a constant emotional buzz in our lives as a result of being His followers. But He is speaking of a love that doesn't lose sight of the very things that brought it into being. When a husband and wife begin to take each other for granted, when their life begins to become a mere routine and the romance is dying, then you can know that marriage is in danger. This can happen to us as believers. We can start taking God for granted. We can start taking church for granted. We can start taking our faith for granted. Sure, we're still going through the motions, but have we left our first love? — Greg Laurie, *For Every Season: Daily Devotions* (Dana Point, CA: Kerygma Publishing—Allen David Books, 2011).

 **5. What were they to do?**

Perhaps we walked with God early in life, or even got all the way through college with our faith intact. But then, through small concessions in our lives, our walk with the Lord began to erode. Little by little we slipped away from the things that once had been important to us.

What should we do today? How do we get back? We must remember from whence we have fallen. Repent where we are. Go back and repeat the first works. Confess our sin.

Acknowledge who we are. And then remember that God loves us.

The good news of the gospel, my friend, is that before the prodigal ever turned his heart toward home, the father had been praying and waiting for him, thinking of what it would be like to embrace him again in his arms.

God will not force Himself upon us. He will not come and drag us out of our situation. But if we will return, He will love us all the way back home. — David Jeremiah, *Sanctuary: Finding Moments of Refuge in the Presence of God* (Nashville, TN: Integrity Publishers, 2002), 282.

**6. Verse 5 says to do the things they did at first. What were those things?**

What were you doing when you were on fire for the Lord?

"I was going to church."

Go again!

"I was getting up early for morning devotions."

Do it again!

"I sang praise to the Lord as I drove down the street."

Sing again!

Remember how it used to be when you were amazed by the Lord's goodness—do again what you were doing then, and you will see the cutting edge return. The injunction of Jesus is simple: Remember, repent, and return. — Jon Courson, *Jon Courson's Application Commentary* (Nashville, TN: Thomas Nelson, 2003), 1671.

**7.** **Notice he does not command them to feel differently. He commands them to do the things they did at first. Why do you think he commands them to do rather than commanding them to feel?**

In times of discouragement, run—don't walk—to the Word of God. You may hear yourself say something like, "I'm too low for Bible-reading today. My heart wouldn't be in it." My friend, that's the point! When your heart is ailing, it needs a transfusion of hope and power. I tell people to learn the principle of force-feeding: Get the book out, open it up, sit yourself down, tune your mind in, and read the Word aloud. These are practical things you can do; don't wait for your feelings, for you can act your way into feeling easier than you can "feel" your way into acting.

I know how hard it can be. I have those mornings when my spirits are at low ebb as I approach my appointment with God. I speak to Him very frankly: "Lord, I need something special from You today. I'm going through a rough place here. I want more than words on a page; more than ideas and spiritual concepts. I need You. I need Your voice. And so I'm asking You to meet me in Your Word today, Lord."

There are also times when I've said, "I refuse to put this Book down until I hear from You, Lord." Don't you think He's pleased by our yearning to know Him? He's going to answer you if you approach with a determined heart. He's going to help you see just what you need to see in His Word, and He's going to give you the grace that will help you prevail through the bumps in the rocky road of life. This is no ordinary book. God's Spirit dwells in its pages, and He yearns for you to find Him in passages like this one:

> God is our refuge and strength,
> A very present help in trouble.
> Therefore we will not fear,

Though the earth be removed,
And though the mountains be carried into the midst of the sea;
Though its waters roar and be troubled,
Though the mountains shake with its swelling. (Psalm 46:1–3)

David Jeremiah, Slaying the Giants in Your Life (Nashville, TN: W Pub., 2001), 32–33.

## 8. Which comes first, behavior or emotion?

There is no substitute for enthusiasm. When the members of a team are enthusiastic, the whole team becomes highly energized. And that energy produces power. Industrialist Charles Schwab observed, "People can succeed at almost anything for which they have enthusiasm."

You cannot win if you do not begin. That's one of the reasons why you need to act your way into feeling. You can't break a cycle of apathy by waiting to feel like doing it. I addressed an issue similar to this in Failing Forward:

> People who want to get out of the fear cycle often . . . believe that they have to eliminate [their fear] to break the cycle. But . . . you can't wait for motivation to get you going. To conquer fear, you have to feel the fear and take action anyway . . . You've got to get yourself moving. The only way to break the cycle is to face your fear and take action—no matter how small or seemingly insignificant that action might seem. To get over fear, you've got to get started.

Likewise, if you want to be enthusiastic, you need to start acting that way. If you wait for the feeling before acting, you may never become enthusiastic. — John C. Maxwell, *The Maxwell Daily Reader: 365 Days of Insight to Develop the*

*Leader within You and Influence Those around You* (Nashville: Thomas Nelson, 2008).

## 9. Revelation 3.14ff. What was the problem in the Laodicean church?

When you are feeling a little under the weather, one of the first things your doctor will want to know is your body temperature. Why? Because a drop or a rise in your temperature is an indication that something is wrong. Your temperature is an assessment of your health.

We can apply the same principle in the spiritual life. What is your spiritual temperature right now? That, too, is an indicator of your health—your spiritual health. According to Scripture, there are only three possible answers, because there are only three possible spiritual temperatures.

The first is burning hot, which means you have a heart that is on fire for God. Remember the story of the two disciples who, although they didn't know it at the time, encountered the risen Lord on the Emmaus road? They said, "Did not our heart burn within us while He talked with us on the road, and while He opened the Scriptures to us?" (Luke 24:32). A burning heart is the best spiritual temperature of all.

The second temperature is cold. Jesus said, "And because lawlessness will abound, the love of many will grow cold" (Matt. 24:12). This would describe someone who is just going through the motions and, for all practical purposes, is spiritually lifeless.

Then there is lukewarm. It may surprise you to know that of the three spiritual temperatures, this is the most offensive to Jesus. In fact, lukewarm is even more offensive to Him than being icy cold. — Greg Laurie, *For Every Season, Volume Two*

(Dana Point, CA: Kerygma Publishing—Allen David Books, 2011).

## 10. What is the lesson for our church?

They were so focused on themselves and their so-called success that they didn't notice who was missing from the assembly: Jesus. To spiritually lukewarm believers, it doesn't matter if Jesus is present or not. They become so caught up with themselves and busy with their agenda that they carry on without Him. And when Jesus does come near, they won't let Him warm their tepid hearts.

Passion for God and his kingdom must move from something we occasionally think about to something we embrace heart and soul. Sue Monk Kidd writes: "I'm discovering that a spiritual journey is a lot like a poem. You don't merely recite a poem or analyze it intellectually. You dance it, sing it, cry it, feel it on your skin and in your bones. You move with it and feel its caress. It falls on you like a teardrop or wraps around you like a smile. It lives in the heart and the body as well as the spirit and the head."

Churches fall into spiritual passivity the same way they lose their passion: one careless believer at a time. If the church today—yours and mine in particular—is going to be a passionate influence on our needy world, it will only happen as individual Christians like you and me throw off the conceit of this age and pursue wholeheartedly an intimate, passionate relationship with Jesus. — David Jeremiah, *Life Wide Open: Unleashing the Power of a Passionate* Life (Nashville: Integrity Publishers, 2003), 87–88.

## 11. Why do you think God used the illustration of being luke-warm with this particular church?

Are you an awakened believer? An on-fire believer? Are you using the gifts and resources that God has given you? I hope so, because we find the sad alternative in the church of Laodicea in Revelation 3.

This church, in contrast to the church in Philadelphia (see Rev. 3:7–12), was not reviving. It was not keeping God's Word. This was a complacent, apathetic, half-hearted, yet very religious church that was hiding behind the veneer of prosperity and wealth and accomplishment. But Jesus gave His diagnosis of their true spiritual condition: "I know all the things you do, that you are neither hot nor cold." (Rev. 3:15 NLT). While the church of Sardis was a cold, dead church, and the church of Philadelphia was hot, alive, and vital, Laodicea was neither cold nor hot. It was merely lukewarm.

Archeologists have made an interesting discovery at Laodicea. They found that it had no local water supply. The city obtained its water through an aqueduct from the hot springs of Hierapolis some six miles away. So let's say, for example, that you were staying in a hotel in ancient Laodicea. If you turned on the faucet, you wouldn't get hot water. You wouldn't get cold water. You would get lukewarm water. Jesus basically told them, "Speaking of that, I think your spiritual condition is lukewarm." He was saying these people were in the middle. They were halfhearted. The lukewarm person has no passion, no enthusiasm, and no urgency for the things of the Spirit. It is a condition in which conviction does not affect the conscience, heart, or will. And it is religion in its worst form. — Greg Laurie, *For Every Season, Volume Two* (Dana Point, CA: Kerygma Publishing—Allen David Books, 2011).

## 12. What do we learn about God from this passage?

Divided allegiance is as wrong as open idolatry. "How long will you hesitate between two opinions?" Elijah asks the people of Israel. The easiest thing to do when you are outnumbered or overwhelmed is to remain in that mediocre state of noncommitment. That was where the people of Israel lived, but Elijah never went there. He told them, "You cannot continue in this period of divided allegiance any longer."

The strongest words that were given to the seven churches mentioned in the book of Revelation, chapters 2 and 3, were given to the church at Laodicea. And the reason is clear: they were uncommitted. They existed in neutrality. "'I know your deeds, that you are neither cold nor hot; I would that you were cold or hot. So because you are lukewarm, and neither hot nor cold, I will spit you out of My mouth'" (Revelation 3:15–16).

Get off the fence of indecision, Elijah told the people of Israel. Either you are for God or against Him.

Perhaps you have known God for many years but have never truly been committed to Him. Now is the time to change that. Stop hiding your love for and commitment to Christ. Let the word out! Tactfully yet fearlessly speak devotedly of your faith. Start now. There are so many strategic ways God can use you in your business, your profession, your school, your neighborhood. You don't agree with the ungodly cultural drift that's happening around you? Say so! You sense an erosion of spirituality at your church, and you're serving in a leadership capacity? Address it! Neutrality in the hour of decision is a curse that invariably leads to tragic consequences.

Our most effective tool is the prayer of faith.

When it came down to the wire, when Baal had failed and God was about to do His work, the one instrument that Elijah employed was prayer. — Charles R. Swindoll, *Great Days with the Great Lives* (Nashville: Thomas Nelson, 2006).

## 13. Verse 18. What do white clothes represent?

Laodiceans would doubt that they were "naked"; their city was famous for its production of textiles, especially cloth and carpets woven from black wool. Thus some commentators observe that Jesus' offer of "white clothes" probably provides a stark contrast with this notorious black wool of Laodicea. They may also experience surprise that they need Jesus to supply them spiritual eye salve. Ancient sources report a first-century medical school located in Laodicea, ear ointment made there, a famous eye doctor practicing there, and eye salve made of Phrygian powder (probably abundantly available there).19 Yet most Laodiceans would acknowledge the usefulness of divine help alongside their medical establishment. Thus the city greatly revered both Apollo, god of prophecy, and Asklepios, god of healing. — Craig S. Keener, *Revelation, The NIV Application Commentary* (Grand Rapids, MI: Zondervan Publishing House, 1999), 160.

## 14. How does Jesus feel about the lukewarm?

The language of 3:17–18 employs the technique of irony common in ancient texts: thus, for example, a blind seer tells a sighted king that he sees but will be blind, and is rich but will become poor; but the metaphor is especially common in the biblical prophets (Isa. 6:10; 29:9; 42:19; 43:8; 56:10; Jer. 5:21; Ezek. 12:2; cf. John 9:39–41). The Laodicean Christians, reflecting the values of their prosperous society, boast, "I am rich and wealthy," as had Israel of old (Hos. 12:8). Jesus advises them to buy true wealth and garments from him

(Rev. 3:18; 21:18, 21; cf. Isa. 55:1), which contrast starkly with the grandeur of the world (Rev. 17:4; 18:12, 16).

Lest anyone misunderstand the tone and motivation of Jesus' rebuke, he makes clear that its purpose is love (3:19, using the language of Prov. 3:12; cf. Heb. 12:6; 1 Clem. 56.4). Indeed, not only does Jesus not reject them, but he wants to have dinner with them (Rev. 3:20), a familiar image for intimacy in antiquity; inviting Jesus in for a meal was the least sort of hospitality one would expect of even an acquaintance. Can a Christian who calls Jesus Lord do any less? The personalized nature of the invitation suggests that not only the future messianic banquet (2:17; 19:9) but a present foretaste of the intimacy available to those who respond to Jesus' call; hearing Jesus' "voice" may perform the same function as in John 10:3–4. Jesus is inviting the Laodicean Christians to realize how they have shut him out of their lives with their own self-sufficiency. — Craig S. Keener, Revelation, *The NIV Application Commentary* (Grand Rapids, MI: Zondervan Publishing House, 1999), 161.

## 15. How do they seem to feel about themselves?

It is easy to see that these people were not troubled with any consciousness of sin. They would never even think of standing afar off with downcast eyes and drooping head, smiting their breast, saying, 'O God, be merciful to me, the sinner'. They had 'arrived'! Hence, to their own way of thinking, they were not in need of any admonition and they could afford to be lukewarm with respect to any exhortation. 'Lukewarm', that is the word. The people of Laodicea knew exactly what that meant. Lukewarm, tepid, flabby, half-hearted, limp, always ready to compromise, indifferent, listless: that 'we're-all-good-people-here-in-Laodicea' attitude. The author of this book has become personally acquainted with this attitude on the part of some church members. You cannot do anything with such people. With the heathen, that is with those who have never come into contact with the gospel and who are therefore 'cold' with respect to it, you can do something. With sincere, humble Christians you can work with joy. But with these 'we're-all-such-very-good-folks-here-in-Laodicea' people you can do nothing. Even Christ Himself cannot stand them. An emotion, a feeling is here ascribed to the Lord which is not predicated of Him anywhere else in the Good Book. We do not read that He is grieved with them. Neither do we read that He is angry with them. No, He is disgusted with these straddlers. And not just slightly disgusted but thoroughly nauseated. 'So because thou art lukewarm, and neither hot nor cold, I will spew thee out of my mouth.' Knowing very well that their entire religion is just so much sham and pretence, so much hypocrisy, the Lord introduces Himself to them as their very opposite: 'These things saith the Amen, the faithful and genuine witness.' In other words, the Lord reveals Himself here as the One whose eyes not only see exactly what is going on in the hearts of these people of Laodicea but whose lips also declare the exact truth as seen. He states, moreover, that He is the 'beginning of the creation of God', that is, the source of the entire creation (cf. 21:6; 22:13; Jn. 1:1; Col. 1:15–18). 'People of Laodicea, you need to become new creatures: you need new hearts. Turn to me, therefore, that ye may be saved.' — William Hendriksen, *More than Conquerors: An Interpretation of the Book of Revelation* (Grand Rapids, MI: Baker Books, 1967), 76–77.

### 16. What do we learn about sin from this passage?

I wonder if we can understand the impact our sin has in heaven. We get a clue in Revelation 3:16 when Jesus threatens to spit the lukewarm church out of his mouth. The verb literally means "to vomit." Their sin, excuse the phrase, made God want to puke. Their acts caused him, not just distaste, but disgust.

Haven't you felt the same? Haven't you witnessed the horror of a human act and wanted to throw up? On last night's news broadcast the story was told of a ten-year-old boy who'd been allegedly set afire by his father. The man had stuffed tissue down his son's T-shirt, covered the boy with lighter fluid, and set him aflame. Why? Because the boy had taken some of the father's food stamps.

Doesn't such a story disgust you? Make you angry? And if we, who are also sinners, have such a reaction, how much more should a holy God? After all, it is his law being broken. His children being abused. His word being ignored.

His holiness being insulted.

The question is not, "Couldn't God overlook sin?" The question instead is, "How in the world is forgiveness an option?" The question is not why God finds it difficult to forgive, but how he finds it possible to do so at all.

From God's angle the tragedy of these men was not that they were about to die, but that they were dying with unresolved sin. They were leaving this earth hostile to God, defiant of his truth, and resistant to his call. "When people's thinking is controlled by the sinful self, they are against God" (Rom. 8:7). Sin is not an unfortunate slip or a regrettable act; it is a posture of defiance against a holy God.

Such is what heaven sees. — Max Lucado, *A Gentle Thunder : Hearing God through the Storm* (Dallas, TX: Word Pub., 1995), 83–84.

## 17. Revelation 3.20. What do we learn about Jesus from this verse?

Jesus always knocks before entering.

He doesn't have to. He owns your heart.

If anyone has the right to barge in, Christ does.

But He doesn't.

That gentle tap you here? It's Christ.

— Max Lucado, *Everyday Blessings: Inspirational Thoughts from the Published Works of Max Lucado.* (Nashville, TN: Thomas Nelson, Inc., 2004).

## 18. What are we to do when we find our hearts lukewarm? How can we keep from being lukewarm?

He said he's knocking. He said if you hear his voice, and if you'll open the door, only then will he come in. But he's not in yet. If you've been lukewarm, if you've been normal or comfortable, he's knocking on your door. He wants you to let him in — all the way in. He desperately wants you to know him. So many people believe in God, but they don't really know him. And because they don't really know him, they are lukewarm. The truth is, if you truly knew him, you couldn't be lukewarm or halfhearted. If you remain lukewarm, maybe it's because you don't know who God really is.

Jesus is the Alpha and the Omega. He is the Beginning and the End. He is the First and the Last. He said, "I am the true vine," "I am the door," "I am the gate," "I am the way, the truth, and the life," "I am the bread of life," "I am the good shepherd." Who is he? He is the one who was humble enough to come riding on a donkey. And yet, when he returns, he will be riding a white horse, wearing a robe dipped in blood. On his thigh will be written, "The King of kings and the Lord of lords." Out of his mouth will come a sword with which to judge the nations. He is the lion and he is the lamb of God. He is the one who was without sin, born in a cave, so that no one would ever feel too low for him. Yet he called the religious people a brood of vipers. They didn't get him. He told the sinners, "I love you." He told the rich it would be hard for them to enter the kingdom of God. He is the one who was beaten and bled and suffered and died and rose again — so that we could have life. — Craig Groeschel, *Weird: Because Normal Isn't Working* (Grand Rapids, MI: Zondervan, 2011).

19. **What do you want to recall from today's discussion?**

20. **How can we support one another in prayer this week?**

# Revelation, Lesson #3
## Good Questions Have Small Groups Talking
### www.joshhunt.com

Email your people and invite them to read this chapter carefully before class. Encourage them to get a Study Bible and read the notes for this chapter. If everyone had a different Study Bible and would read it before class, you could really have a great conversation!

## Revelation 4

### OPEN

Let's each share your name and who is the most powerful person you have ever met?

### DIG

1. **Overview. Circle every occurrence of the word "throne" in this chapter.**

   The key word in this chapter is throne; it is used fourteen times. In fact, this is a key word in the entire book, appearing forty-six times. No matter what may happen on earth, God is on His throne and is in complete control. Various teachers interpret Revelation in different ways, but all agree that John is emphasizing the glory and sovereignty of God. What an encouragement that would be to the suffering saints of John's day and of every age in history.

   Using the throne as the focal point, we can easily understand the arrangement of this exciting chapter.

On the throne—Almighty God (vv. 2-3a). This is God the Father, since the Son approaches the throne in Revelation 5:6, and the Spirit is pictured before the throne in Revelation 4:5. There is no possible way for human words to describe what God is like in His essence. John can only use comparisons. Jasper is a clear gem (see Rev. 21:11) and the sardine is red. The Lord is robed in light, according to Psalm 104:2 and 1 Timothy 6:16. Both the jasper and the sardius (sardine) were found in the breastplate of the high priest (Ex. 28:17-21).

Around the throne—a rainbow (v. 3b). This rainbow was a complete circle, not merely an arc, for in heaven all things are completed. The rainbow reminds us of God's covenant with Noah (Gen. 9:11-17), symbolic of His promise that He would never again destroy the earth with a flood. God's covenant, as we shall see, was not only with Noah, but with all of His creation.

Judgment is about to fall, but the rainbow reminds us that God is merciful, even when He judges (Hab. 3:2). Usually, a rainbow appears after the storm; but here, we see it before the storm.

Around the throne—elders and living creatures (vv. 3-4, 6-7). The rainbow was around the throne vertically, while these heavenly beings were around the throne horizontally. They are, as it were, the king's court.

Who are these twenty-four elders seated on thrones? It is unlikely that they are angels, because angels are not numbered (Heb. 12:22), crowned, or enthroned. Besides, in Revelation 7:11, the elders are distinguished from the angels (see also Rev. 5:8-11). The crowns they wear are the "victor's crowns" (the Greek word Stephanos; see Rev. 2:10); and we have no evidence that angels receive rewards. — *The Bible Exposition Commentary – New Testament, Volume 2.*

2. **Verse 1 mentions a door. Can you think of other doors in Heaven?**

In the early chapters of the Revelation there are three of the most important doors in life.

(i) There is the door of opportunity. "Behold," said the Risen Christ to the Church at Philadelphia, "I have set before you an open door" (Rev 3:8). That was the door of the glorious opportunity by which the message of the gospel could be taken to the regions beyond. God sets before every man his own door of opportunity.

(ii) There is the door of the human heart. "Behold," says the Risen Christ, "I stand at the door and knock (Rev 3:20). At the door of every heart there comes the knock of the nail-pierced hand, and a man may open or refuse to open.

(iii) There is the door of revelation. "I saw a door in heaven standing open," says the seer. God offers to every man the door which leads to the knowledge of God and of life eternal. — *Barclay's Daily Study Bible (NT)*.

3. **Revelation 4.1, 2. What do we learn about God from these verses?**

One of my favorite verses is Revelation 4:2 (NIV) "And there before me was a throne in heaven with someone sitting on it."

Sitting.

Not wringing his hands. Not pacing the floor. Sitting. Large and in charge. In control. Working out Romans 8:28. Making every day a Romans 8.28 day. — Josh Hunt, *Obedience*, 2013.

### 4. What is God doing sitting there on the throne?

Want to see a great example of the truth of Romans 8:28? Look at the life of Joseph. He was hated by his brothers, sold into slavery, falsely accused, thrown in jail, and became the savior of his family. God was working out his plan.

I have often felt that way about my life. I was a Minister of Education for eleven years. My job satisfaction was about a five on a scale of one to ten. There were parts of it I loved and parts I hated. It was during this era I started writing Bible study lessons called Good Questions Have Groups Talking. I wrote my first book during this era. This was the part I liked. I was also asked to do my first training conference during this era. I liked that part too. All the rest I didn't like so well.

A few years later I was doing conferences full-time. I have logged two million miles on American Airlines alone. I liked speaking, but I was about half bored. My in-laws' church needed a pastor and they called me. It would have been the last place I would ever have considered. But God was working out his plan. It is a really country situation and I have never considered myself a country boy. But it has worked out well. I get to preach every week and because the church is so small, there is not much else that needs to be done. God was working out his plan.

God is always working out his plan. Through twists and turns and setbacks and heartaches and detours and roadblocks, God is working out his plan. — Josh Hunt, *Obedience*, 2013.

### 5. We always want to read the Bible for application. What is the application of this verse? What difference does it make?

When it sometimes feels this world is careening recklessly out of control, it is nice to know there is someone in the throne room of the universe and he is sitting down. He is not wringing his hands. He is not pacing the floor. The throne is occupied. Praise God. All is well. All is as it should be. There is a throne in heaven and someone is sitting on it. — Josh Hunt, *You Can Double Your Church In Five Years or Less,* 2000.

6.  **Verse 3. What does the rainbow represent? What does it teach us about God? Can you think of other rainbows in the Bible?**

The throne of God is surrounded by the rainbow, sign of the Noachic covenant and therefore of peace. Here is one of the things we can know for certain about God: he intends peace for his creatures. The tableau that unfolds before us is the well-ordered cosmos, creation as it ought to be; even the sea—in Israel's imagination the source of disorder and chaos—appears here as tamed, a smooth, glassy sea spreading out before the throne (4:6). After the flood comes the rainbow that seals the covenant. Nowhere is this rainbow more vividly depicted than in William Blake's watercolor The four and Twenty Elders Casting Their Crowns before the Divine Throne, which art critic Morton Paley cites as a rare instance of "the apocalyptic beautiful" genre. This is one answer to those who equate apocalyptic only with themes of gloom, doom, and destruction. The apocalyptic imagination encompasses the harmony and unity of creation as it is fulfilled beyond the horrors of this age. God created all things good in the beginning, and he will finish what he has begun. — Joseph L. Mangina, *Revelation, Brazos Theological Commentary on the Bible* (Grand Rapids, MI: Brazos Press, 2010), 76–77.

7.  **Verse 4. Who are these elders? What do the robes teach us?**

These elders probably symbolize the people of God in heaven, enthroned and rewarded. There were twenty-four courses of priests in the Old Testament temple (1 Chron. 24:3-5, 18; see also Luke 1:5-9). God's people are "kings and priests" (Rev. 1:6), reigning and serving with Christ. Note especially their praise (Rev. 5:9-10). When Daniel (Dan. 7:9) saw the thrones set up (not "cast down" as in the King James Version), they were empty; but when John saw them, they had been filled. Since there were twelve tribes of Israel and twelve Apostles, perhaps the number twenty-four symbolizes the completion of God's people.

The white robes and palm branches speak of victory (see Rev. 7:9). These are the "overcomers" who have conquered because of their faith in Christ (1 John 5:4-5). — *The Bible Exposition Commentary – New Testament, Volume 2.*

8. **Notice these elders are sitting on thrones. I would have expected there was only one throne in Heaven—God's. This reminds me of 2 Timothy 2.12. What does this verse teach we will be doing in Heaven?**

I think the average Christian sees Heaven is an eternal retirement home. That is not biblical. Heaven will be a very active place. There will be places to go and people to see and things to do. I say this reverently: Heaven will be fun. I wouldn't be surprised to see motorcycles and snow skiing and tennis. There won't be golf. It couldn't be heaven if there were golf. Too frustrating!

Our God is a God of productivity and Heaven will be a place of doing. Our God is a creative God and Heaven will be a creative place. We will build things, draw things, and make art and music. Joni Eareckson Tada says, "All the earthly things we enjoy with our friends here will find their more exalted expression in heaven."

We will have renewed minds, as well as renewed bodies. We will be people full of energy and clearheaded thinking. Our vision and hearing will be perfect. We will be eager to take on new projects and will have the energy to complete them. Whatever a great day at work feels like for you, Heaven will be a little bit like that. We will exercise leadership and authority in making important decisions. We will have ideas and the energy to carry out those ideas.

Heaven will be a place of rest. God gives a pattern for rest. He created the world in six days, and on the seventh day, He rested. Heaven will include both work and rest.

The rest of Heaven will be different than the rest here. It will be totally relaxing. We will be able to sit down by a river and not think about work. In Heaven, rest will be worry-free. — Brandon Park, *After Life* (Pulpit Press, 2014).

9. **Again, read for application. What is the application of this for us? What does this teach us about ourselves?**

In God's book man is heading somewhere. He has an amazing destiny. We are being prepared to walk down the church aisle and become the bride of Jesus. We are going to live with him. Share the throne with him. Reign with him. We count. We are valuable. And what's more, our worth is built in! Our value is inborn.

You see, if there was anything that Jesus wanted everyone to understand it was this: A person is worth something simply because he is a person. That is why he treated people like he did. Think about it. The girl caught making undercover thunder with someone she shouldn't—he forgave her. The untouchable leper who asked for cleansing—he touched him. And the blind welfare case that cluttered the roadside—he honored him. And the worn-out old windbag addicted to self-pity near the pool of Siloam—he healed him! — *No Wonder They Call Him the Savior* / Max Lucado, *Grace for the Moment® Volume Ii: More Inspirational Thoughts for Each Day of the Year* (Nashville: Thomas Nelson, 2006).

## 10. Verse 5. What do these flashes of lightening teach us?

Out of the throne—storm signals (v. 5a). "And from the throne proceed flashes of lightning and sounds and peals of thunder" (nasb). These are indications of a coming storm and reminders of God's awesome power (see Ex. 9:23, 28; 19:16). These "storm signals" will be repeated during the time of judgment, always proceeding from the throne and temple of God (Rev. 8:5; 11:19; 16:18). God has indeed prepared His throne for judgment (Ps. 9:7; note also 77:18).

Our world does not like to think of God as a God of judgment. They prefer to look at the rainbow around the throne and ignore the lightning and thunder out of the throne. He certainly is a God of grace, but His grace reigns through righteousness (Rom. 5:21). This was made clear at the cross where God manifested both His love for sinners and His wrath against sin. — *The Bible Exposition Commentary – New Testament, Volume 2.*

## 11. Verse 6. What do these creatures represent?

Also around the throne, John saw four "living creatures" ("beasts" in the King James Version) who were nearer to God than the angels and the elders. They resemble the cherubim that the Prophet Ezekiel saw (Ezek. 1:4-14; 10:20-22), but their praise (Rev. 4:8) reminds us of the seraphim of Isaiah 6. I believe that these special creatures symbolize God's creation and are related to God's covenant with Noah (Gen. 9:8-17). The faces of the living creatures parallel God's statement in Genesis 9:10—His covenant is with Noah (the face of the man), the fowl (the face of the eagle), the cattle (the face of the calf), and the beasts of the earth (the face of the lion).

These creatures signify the wisdom of God ("full of eyes") and proclaim the holiness of God. They are heavenly reminders that God has a covenant with His creation and that He rules His creation from His throne. The presence of the emerald rainbow further enhances this image, since the rainbow was given as the sign of the creation covenant. No matter what terrible judgments may fall on God's earth, He will be faithful to keep His Word. Men may curse Him during the judgments (Rev. 16:9, 11, 21), but nature will praise Him and magnify His holiness.

The cherubim described in Ezekiel 1 seem to have a part in the providential workings of God in the world, pictured by the "wheels within the wheels." God uses the forces of nature to accomplish His will (Ps. 148), and all nature praises and thanks Him. — *The Bible Exposition Commentary – New Testament, Volume 2.*

## 12. This is slightly off topic, but… do you think there will be animals in Heaven? Do you think there will be pets? Do all dogs go to Heaven? ;-)

Talk about a question that stirs up emotion! The suggestion that there will not be pets in heaven has caused more than a few animal lovers to get downright squirrely. There is, however, no need to go nuts. While Scripture does not answer the question about pets in heaven conclusively, there is ample reason to think that animals will inhabit paradise restored.

First, animals populated the garden of Eden. Thus, there is a precedent for believing that animals will populate Eden restored, as well. Animals are among God's most creative creations. Thus, it would seem incredible that he would banish such wonders in paradise restored. Says philosopher Peter Kreeft, "How irrational is the prejudice that would allow plants (green fields and flowers) but not animals into Heaven!"

Furthermore, while we cannot say for certain that the pets we enjoy today will be "resurrected" in eternity, I for one am not willing to preclude the possibility. Some of the keenest thinkers from Joni Eareckson Tada to Peter Kreeft to C. S. Lewis are not only convinced that animals in general, but pets in particular, will be restored in the new heavens and the new earth. If God resurrected our pets it would be in total keeping with his overwhelming grace and goodness.

Finally, the Scriptures from first to last suggest that animals have souls. Moses in Genesis and John in Revelation communicate that the Creator endowed animals with souls (Genesis 1:20; Revelation 8:9). However, because the soul of an animal is qualitatively different from the soul of a human, there is reasonable doubt that it can survive the death of its body.

One thing is certain: Scripture provides us with sufficient precedence for believing that animals will inhabit the new heaven and new earth. In the words of Isaiah, "The wolf will live with the lamb, the leopard will lie down with the goat, the calf and the lion and the yearling together; and a little child will lead them" (Isaiah 11:6–9). — Hank Hanegraaff, *Afterlife: What You Really Want to Know about Heaven* (Brentwood, TN: Worthy Publishing, 2013).

### 13. What do we learn about God and His home in Heaven from the sea of glass?

There are three things that this sea like shining glass does symbolize.

(i) It symbolizes preciousness. In the ancient world glass was usually dull and semi-opaque, and glass as clear as crystal was as precious as gold. In Job 28:17 gold and glass are mentioned together as examples of precious things.

(ii) It symbolizes dazzling purity. The blinding light reflected from the glassy sea would be too much for the eyes to look upon, like the purity of God.

(iii) It symbolizes immense distance. The throne of God was in the immense distance, as if at the other side of a great sea. Swete writes of "the vast distance which, even in the case of one who stood in the door of heaven, intervened between himself and the throne of God."

One of the greatest characteristics of the writing of the seer is the reverence which, even in the heavenly places, never dares to be familiar with God, but paints its picture in terms of light and distance. — *Barclay's Daily Study Bible (NT)*.

## 14. Verse 8. What is the primary activity of Heaven?

True spiritual worship is perhaps one of the greatest needs in our individual lives and in our churches. There is a constant emphasis today on witnessing for Christ and working for Christ, but not enough is said about worshiping Him. To worship means "to ascribe worth" (see Rev. 4:11; 5:12). It means to use all that we are and have to praise God for all that He is and does.

Heaven is a place of worship, and God's people shall worship Him throughout all eternity. Perhaps it would be good for us to get in practice now! A study of Revelation 4-5 will certainly help us better understand how to worship God and give Him the glory that He deserves. — The Bible Exposition Commentary – New Testament, Volume 2.

### 15. What exactly does it mean that God is holy, holy, holy?

As used in Scripture, holiness describes both the majesty of God and the purity and moral perfection of His nature. Holiness is one of His attributes; that is, holiness is an essential part of the nature of God. His holiness is as necessary as His existence, or as necessary, for example, as His wisdom or omniscience. Just as He cannot but know what is right, so He cannot but do what is right.

We ourselves do not always know what is right, what is just and fair. At times we agonize over decisions having moral overtones. "What is the right thing to do?" we ask. God, of course, never faces this predicament. His perfect knowledge precludes any uncertainty on what is right and wrong.

But sometimes, even when we know what is right there is a reluctance on our part to do it. The right action may involve sacrifice, or a blow to our pride (for example, when we know we should confess a sin to someone), or some other obstacle. But here again, this is never true with God. God never vacillates. He always does what is just and right without the slightest hesitation. It is impossible in the very nature of God for Him to do otherwise.

God's holiness then is perfect freedom from all evil. We say a garment is clean when it is free from any spot, or gold is pure when all dross has been refined from it. In this manner we can think of the holiness of God as the absolute absence of any evil in Him. John said, "God is light; in him there is no darkness at all" (1 John 1:5). Light and darkness, when used this way in Scripture, have moral significance. John is telling us that God is absolutely free from any moral evil and that He is Himself the essence of moral purity.

The holiness of God also includes His perfect conformity to His own divine character. That is, all of His thoughts and actions are consistent with His holy character. By contrast, consider our own lives. Over time, as we mature in the Christian life, we develop a certain degree of Christian character. We grow in such areas as truthfulness, purity, and humility. But we do not always act consistently with our character. We tell a lie or allow ourselves to get trapped into a series of impure thoughts. Then we are dismayed with ourselves for these actions because they are inconsistent with our character. This never happens to God. He always acts consistently with His holy character. And it is this standard of holiness that God has called us to when He says, "Be holy, because I am holy." — Jerry Bridges, *The Pursuit of Holiness* (Colorado Springs: Navpress, 1978), 22–24.

## 16. Again, application. What difference does it make that God is holy, holy, holy?

The absolute holiness of God should be of great comfort and assurance to us. If God is perfectly holy, then we can be confident that His actions toward us are always perfect and just. We are often tempted to question God's actions and complain that He is unfair in His treatment of us. This is the devil's lie, the same thing he did to Eve. He essentially told her, "God is being unfair to you" (Genesis 3:4–5). But it is impossible in the very nature of God that He should ever be unfair. Because He is holy, all His actions are holy.

We must accept by faith the fact that God is holy, even when trying circumstances make it appear otherwise. To complain against God is in effect to deny His holiness and to say He is not fair. In the seventeenth century Stephen Charnock said, "It is less injury to Him to deny His being, than to deny the purity of it; the one makes Him no God, the other a deformed, unlovely, and a detestable God...he that saith God is not holy speaks much worse than he that saith there is no God at all."

I still vividly recall how God first dealt with me over twenty-five years ago about complaining against Him. In response to His will, I had settled in San Diego, California, and had begun to look for a job. When several weeks went by without success, I mentally began to accuse God. "After all, I gave up my plans to do His will and now He has let me down." God graciously directed my attention to Job 34:18–19: "Is he not the One who says to kings, 'You are worthless,' and to nobles, 'You are wicked,' who shows no partiality to princes and does not favor the rich over the poor, for they are all the work of his hands?" As soon as I read that passage I immediately fell to my knees confessing to Him my terrible sin of complaining and questioning His holiness. God mercifully forgave and the next day I received two job offers. — Jerry Bridges, *The Pursuit of Holiness* (Colorado Springs: Navpress, 1978), 24–25.

## 17. 1 Peter 1.16. What did Peter teach that God's holiness required of us?

But God demands more than that we acknowledge His holiness. He says to us, "Be holy, because I am holy." God rightfully demands perfect holiness in all of His moral creatures. It cannot be otherwise. He cannot possibly ignore or approve of any evil committed. He cannot for one moment relax His perfect standard of holiness. Rather He must say, as He does say, "So be holy in all you do." The Prophet Habakkuk declared, "Your eyes are too pure to look on evil; you cannot tolerate wrong" (Habakkuk 1:13). Because God is holy, He can never excuse or overlook any sin we commit, however small it may be.

Sometimes we try to justify to God some action which our own conscience calls into question. But if we truly grasp the significance of God's perfect holiness, both in Himself and in His demands of us, we will readily see we can never justify before Him even the slightest deviation from His perfect will. God does not accept the excuse, "Well, that's just the way I am," or even the more hopeful statement, "Well, I'm still growing in that area of my life."

No, God's holiness does not make allowance for minor flaws or shortcomings in our personal character. Well might we Christians, though justified solely through the righteousness of Christ, ponder carefully the words of the writer to the Hebrews: "Make every effort...to be holy; without holiness no one will see the Lord" (Hebrews 12:14). — Jerry Bridges, *The Pursuit of Holiness* (Colorado Springs: Navpress, 1978), 26.

## 18. Verse 10. What did the elders understand that we need to remember and never forget?

Much of humanity's trouble stems from our naturally insatiable self-centeredness. We often see ourselves as the center of the universe and tend to describe all other components in reference to us rather than God. The human psyche almost invariably processes incoming information in relationship to its own ego. For example, if the news forecasts an economic slump, the natural hearer automatically processes what it could mean to self, how it affects me, my family, my situation in life. While this response is natural, in perpetual practice this self-absorption is miserable. In some ways our egocentrism is a secret lust for omnipotence. We want to be our own god and have all power. Our first reaction upon hearing this bit of truth might be to deny it—that we've never had a desire to be God. But how often do we take immediate responsibility for handling most of the problems in our midst? How often do we try changing the people we know and feeding our control addiction with the drug of manipulation? Simply put, we try to play God, and frankly, it's exhausting. But thankfully, those of us who are redeemed are also given what 1 Corinthians 2:16 calls the "mind of Christ." Life takes on a far more accurate estimation and perspective when we learn to view it increasingly through the vantage point of the One who spoke it into existence. Think of some of your greatest challenges. Picture them. Then go back and stamp the words "before the throne" in front each of these challenges. The heart of prayer is moving these very kinds of tests and trials from the insecurities and uncertainties of earth to the throne of God. Only then can they be viewed with dependable accuracy and boundless hope. Close your eyes and do your best to picture the glorious seraphim never ceasing to cry, "Holy, holy, holy!" Imagine the lightning emitting from the throne, and hear the rumblings and the thunder. Picture the elders overwhelmed by God's worthiness, casting their crowns before the throne. Approach the throne of grace with confidence, with eyes on Him, not on yourself. Our God is huge! Our God is able! — Beth Moore, *Portraits of Devotion* (Nashville: B&H, 2014).

### 19. What do we learn about our purpose in life from verse 11?

Did you catch that? According to these elders, we exist to bring God glory and pleasure. That is the meaning of life. It is something your iPhone will never tell you. We exist to bring God glory and pleasure. Now if that's true, then we have to face another simple fact: We don't exist to bring ourselves glory and pleasure. So no matter what 61 percent of Americans—or even 50 percent of born-again Christians— might say, the main purpose of life cannot be seeking our own enjoyment and personal fulfillment.

In fact, if I live for pleasure, I will never find it. Let me repeat that: If I live for pleasure, I will never find it. The

Bible says in 1 Timothy 5:6 that "she who is self-indulgent is dead even while she lives."[12] The fact of the matter is that self-indulgence, living for pleasure, is one of the least pleasurable things a person can do. In fact, it has been said that the best cure for hedonism is an attempt to practice it. I believe it.

Freddie Mercury was the lead singer of the rock band Queen, which has sold between 150 million and 300 million records. Members of this group, needless to say, were awash in cash and fame. They had it all. And Mercury had the opportunity, as few ever have had, to devote his life to the pursuit of pleasure. In fact, one of his friends, Elton John, said that Mercury was the only person who could out-party him. Mercury's appetites were unquenchable. In an interview, he was quoted as saying, "Excess is a part of my nature. To me dullness is a disease. I need danger and excitement. . . . Straight people bore me stiff. I love freaky people."[13]

Mercury did not deny himself anything . . . sexually or materially. But it didn't turn out well. And it never does. He realized that in his attempt to be a star, he had effectively created a monster. He later said, "The monster is me. Success, family, money, sex, drugs, whatever you want I can have it. But now I am beginning to see that as much as I created it I want to escape from it. I am starting to worry that I can't control it as much as it controls me."[14] Mercury lost his fight with the monster. He died from complications due to AIDS at the age of forty-five.

The pursuit of pleasure apart from God is indeed a monster. When God saw trouble developing in the heart of Cain, the Lord issued him a warning. Here is my paraphrase of Genesis 4:7: "Sin is lying at your door like a crouching beast. Its desire is for you, but you should rule over it." Sin is like a crouching beast ready to pounce on you—ready to control you—and if you live for pleasure, that beast is going to take over. — Greg Laurie, *As It Is in Heaven: How Eternity Brings Focus to What Really Matters* (Carol Stream, IL: Tyndale, 2014).

### 20. Summary. Think of the average man on the street. How does this view of God differ from his view of God?

We live in a day of pitifully shallow concepts of God. Some of today's contemporary Christian music leaves the impression that God is our buddy—a great pal to have in a pinch. . . . One pop song asks, "What if God were just a slob like us?" That is not the biblical view of God. That is man's feeble attempt to make God relevant.

Do you hear the cheap twang of such a concept of God? These small ideas of Him diminish the beauty of His holiness. . . .

The Puritans, that rigorous people of old, possessed a solidly biblical concept of God. Do you know why it is so crucial for us to recover such a respectful understanding? Because a shallow view of God leads to a shallow life. Cheapen God and you cheapen life itself. Treat God superficially, and you become superficial. — *Moses: A Man of Selfless Dedication* / Charles R. Swindoll, *Wisdom for the Way: Wise Words for Busy People* (Nashville: Thomas Nelson, 2007).

### 21. To close our time together, let me read a prayer. You pray as I read.

We come before You, our Father, and we acknowledge that it is Your holiness that draws us to You. And it is that lack of holiness in ourselves that brings from within us such a hunger to know You better. We affirm with Paul that our determined purpose is that we may know You. That we may progressively become more intimately acquainted with You.

God, that is what we want. More important, that is what we need.

In a culture that's adrift and in a world that's broken, there is something about Your character that guides us and restores us. Your holiness warms our hearts and breaks our stubborn wills. And we stand before You, our holy God, acknowledging that You are pristine, free of corruption, without a hint of sin or transgression.

We are reproved by Your command: "Be holy, for I am holy." The angels acknowledge You by saying, "Holy, holy, holy is the Lord God, the Almighty." You are high and lifted up. You have full perspective and understanding. Your character is unflawed, and we are lost in the wonder of it. We are caught up in the perfection of Your person.

We've never known a Father like You, as good as our fathers may have been. We've never known One so full of compassion and grace and love and mercy. Introduce us again to who You are. Remind us of it again and again, especially when we fail and see ourselves so unworthy. Remind us that none of that blocks Your wondrous forgiveness. Thank You. Thank You.

In the matchless name of Jesus, Your Son and our Savior, we pray. Amen. — Charles Swindoll, *Hear Me When I Call: Learning to Connect with a God Who Cares* (Brentwood, TN: Worthy Publishing, 2013).

# Revelation, Lesson #4
## Good Questions Have Small Groups Talking
### www.joshhunt.com

## Revelation 5

## OPEN
Let's each share your name and what is the best Christian concert you have ever attended?

## DIG
**1. Overview. How is God pictured in this passage?**

We stood and stared at the letter as it lay on the doormat. It was a smart envelope, good quality paper, with clear, bold typewritten name and address. And at the top, in even larger letters, we saw the words: TO BE OPENED BY ADDRESSEE ONLY. And the addressee was not at home. We hardly dared touch it.

But supposing the envelope had said, TO BE OPENED BY THE PERSON WHO DESERVES TO DO SO? That would have been even more intriguing, and would have posed a different kind of challenge. How do you know if you deserve to open it? As one writer put it, we are all overdrawn at the moral bank. The thought of being sufficiently 'deserving' for any task at once makes us search our consciences and discover, no doubt, all kinds of things which might well disqualify us for whatever task is at hand.

That is the situation at the start of this scene. We are still looking, through John's eyes, at the heavenly throne room, and it is not simply one long round of endless, repetitive praise. This is the throne room of God the creator, and his world is not merely a tableau, a living picture to be enjoyed. It is a project. It is going somewhere. There is work to be done.

In particular, there is work to be done to rescue the creation from the deadly dangers that have taken root within it. There is work to be done to overthrow the forces that are out to destroy the very handiwork of God. That will be a terrible task, and one might well shrink from it in itself. But of course we have all made it worse by being, ourselves, part of the problem rather than part of the solution.

This is at the heart of the challenge issued by the 'strong angel' of verse 2. God, the creator, has a scroll in his right hand, like an architect with a rolled-up design for a building, or a general with a rolled-up plan of a campaign. The scroll is sealed with seven seals. We rightly guess, however, that it contains God's secret plan to undo and overthrow the world-destroying projects that have already gained so much ground, and to plant and nurture instead the world-rescuing project which will get creation itself back on track in the right direction. Is there anybody out there who deserves to open this scroll? Is there anybody who has not, themselves, contributed in some way to the problems of creation, to the age-old spoiling and trashing of God's beautiful world? — Tom Wright, *Revelation for Everyone, For Everyone Bible Study Guides* (London; Louisville, KY: SPCK; Westminster John Knox, 2011), 51–52.

## 2. Revelation 5.1. What is the scroll?

On the right hand of the Father lies a scroll (cf. 6:14). It represents God's eternal plan, His decree which is all-comprehensive. It symbolizes God's purpose with respect to the entire universe throughout history, and concerning all creatures in all ages and to all eternity. It is full of writing on both sides. — William Hendriksen, *More than Conquerors: An Interpretation of the Book of Revelation* (Grand Rapids, MI: Baker Books, 1967), 89.

### 3. What do the seals represent?

This scroll is pictured as being entirely sealed with seven seals. These seals were probably arranged in a row on the outside of the scroll. Thus viewed, they sealed the scroll's enclosure. The meaning is this: the closed scroll indicates the plan of God unrevealed and unexecuted. If that scroll remains sealed God's purposes are not realized; His plan is not carried out. To open that scroll by breaking the seals means not merely to reveal but to carry out God's plan. Because of this, a strong angel proclaims with a loud voice, 'Who is worthy to open the scroll or to break its seals?' The voice is loud and strong so that every creature in the entire universe may hear. — William Hendriksen, *More than Conquerors: An Interpretation of the Book of Revelation* (Grand Rapids, MI: Baker Books, 1967), 89.

### 4. Is this the same as the book of life?

This is not the "book of life" (Revelation 20:12), or the "Lamb's book of life" (Revelation 21:27). That book contains the names of those who are redeemed by Jesus, the Lamb of God. This sealed book, about to be opened, contains the circumstances of redemption, portrayed in a highly symbolic way for those who have spiritual eyes to see them. — Lerry W. Fogle, *Revelation Explained* (South Plainfield, NJ: Bridge Publishing, 1981), 146.

### 5. What does it suggest that no one could open the seals?

The fact that the book was sealed meant that its content was established. It was written and was not to be changed, though it was about to be revealed. The sealing process has always been done to secure a matter and make it established. When Daniel was placed in the lion's den, King Nebuchadnezzar had a great stone placed over the mouth of the den and then sealed it with his own seal "that the purpose might not be changed concerning Daniel" (Daniel 6:16–17). In the same way, God had sealed this book with seven complete seals to signify that nothing in it could be changed. God had established it, and it would come to pass. — Lerry W. Fogle, *Revelation Explained* (South Plainfield, NJ: Bridge Publishing, 1981), 145–146.

## 6. Why the weeping?

No-one in the entire universe—heaven, earth, under the earth—was able to open the scroll or even to look inside. As a result John weeps audibly. You will understand the meaning of these tears if you constantly bear in mind that in this beautiful vision the opening of the scroll by breaking the seals indicates the execution of God's plan. When the scroll is opened and the seals are broken, then the universe is governed in the interest of the Church. Then, God's glorious, redemptive purpose is being realized; His plan is being carried out and the contents of the scroll come to pass in the history of the universe. But if the scroll is not opened it means that there will be no protection for God's children in the hours of bitter trial; no judgments upon a persecuting world; no ultimate triumph for believers; no new heaven and earth; no future inheritance. — William Hendriksen, *More than Conquerors: An Interpretation of the Book of Revelation* (Grand Rapids, MI: Baker Books, 1967), 89.

## 7. Verse 6 is clearly a picture of Jesus. What do we learn about Jesus from this verse?

Before we discuss the worthiness of Jesus, we should note the position from which Jesus emerges in this scene. He was "in the midst of the throne and of the four beasts" (5:6). In other words, He was "one" with God. He wasn't even seen until He came forth from the midst of the heavenly throne. He was seated there, exalted at the right hand of God the Father (Ephesians 1:20–23), yet He did not overshadow the Father. Jesus has been manifested to us as part of the Trinity, and we should not forget that He is God. He, the Father and the Spirit are One. — Lerry W. Fogle, *Revelation Explained* (South Plainfield, NJ: Bridge Publishing, 1981), 148–149.

8. **Verses 5, 6. How is Jesus like a lion? How is He like a lamb?**

But here the central paradox of Revelation and of Christian faith in general comes to the fore: Jesus conquered not by force but by death, not by violence but by martyrdom. The Lion is a Lamb! Regularly in ancient literature, lions functioned as images of great strength—the courageous, powerful rulers of the animal kingdom (cf. Rev. 9:8, 17; 10:3). Even Jewish texts use the image of a lion for courage and power in general more often than specifically for the Messiah.11 John turns, expecting to witness a powerful hero. Yet the Lamb, by contrast, provides an image of helplessness. Lambs were the most vulnerable of sheep, and sheep were among the weakest of creatures, typically contrasted with predators.13

Most significantly for John, this is a slaughtered lamb, a sacrificed lamb. Plagues will fall on the disobedient world (Rev. 6–16), but just as the blood of the Passover lamb delivered Israel from the climactic plague (Ex. 12:23), so Jesus' blood will protect his people during God's judgments on humanity (Rev. 7:3). Jesus' victory is like a new exodus (5:9–10; 15:3), and Jesus himself is the new Lamb (cf. 1 Cor. 5:7). — Craig S. Keener, *Revelation, The NIV Application*

*Commentary* (Grand Rapids, MI: Zondervan Publishing House, 1999), 186–187.

**9. Jesus is both lion and lamb. What is the application? What does it mean for us to behave Christianly?**

There have been, down the years, plenty of lion-Christians. Yes, they think, Jesus died for us; but now God's will is to be done in the lion-like fashion, through brute force and violence, to make the world come into line, to enforce God's will. No, replies John; think of the lion, yes, but gaze at the lamb.

And there have been plenty of lamb-Christians. Yes, they think, Jesus may have been 'the lion of Judah', but that's a political idea which we should reject because salvation consists in having our sins wiped away so that we can get out of this compromised world and go off to heaven instead. No, replies John; gaze at the lamb, but remember that it is the lion's victory that he has won.

And remember, as we listen and look, that the lamb has seven horns and seven eyes. He is, that is to say, all-powerful and all-seeing. And he has the right to take the scroll and open it. Everything else follows from this moment. — Tom Wright, *Revelation for Everyone, For Everyone Bible Study Guides* (London; Louisville, KY: SPCK; Westminster John Knox, 2011), 54.

**10. What do you think the horns represent?**

What do the "horns" (5:6) mean? One might speak of horned lambs in apocalyptic symbolism (1 En. 90:9), but horns also appear on literal Passover lambs (tos. Pisha 6:7—though male lambs would grow two horns, not seven). John's reinterpretation of traditional symbolism goes beyond any models of his contemporaries, however, to communicate a uniquely Christian viewpoint. Horns in prophetic literature sometimes represent power (Dan. 7:7–24; 8:3–22), but here the power is not human power, but the seven spirits of God (Rev. 5:6); this alludes to the ancient prophecy that the Jewish king must prevail not by human strength but by the power of the Spirit (Zech. 4:6).-- Craig S. Keener, *Revelation, The NIV Application Commentary* (Grand Rapids, MI: Zondervan Publishing House, 1999), 187.

## 11. And the eyes?

John identifies the horns here with seven eyes (5:6), which he probably understands as representing the Spirit in Zechariah's vision (Zech. 3:9; 4:6, 10) as well as the seven lamps (4:2; Rev. 4:5). But in Zechariah, the eyes that watch over God's purposes and his people belong to God himself; their application to Jesus the Lamb provides a clue to Jesus' true, exalted identity. Jesus' location by the throne (Rev. 5:6) may also suggest a status that some texts reserve for divine Wisdom (Wisd. 9:4; cf. 3 En. 10:1); but Jesus' status is higher even than divine Wisdom, for he ultimately sits in the midst of the throne, sharing the Father's supreme reign (Rev. 7:17; 22:1, 3; though cf. also 3:21). — Craig S. Keener, Revelation, *The NIV Application Commentary* (Grand Rapids, MI: Zondervan Publishing House, 1999), 187.

## 12. Verse 9ff. What is the emotion of this passage?

Think of it as another visit to the theatre. You are sitting in the dark when the drum begins. A slow, steady rhythm. It's telling you something. It's going somewhere. It builds up, louder and louder. Then the voices join in. Wild, excited singing, rich and vivid. That too builds up, louder and louder. Then, as the stage lights come on, the musicians join in as well: the rich brass, the shimmering strings, the sharp, clear oboe and the flute fluttering like a bird to and fro over the top of it all. The music is designed to set the scene, to open the play, to make you realize that this is drama like you've never seen it before.

And the actors? Now for the shock. John, in describing this scene, has hinted that we are the actors. We are listening to the music so that we can now come on stage, ready or not, and play our part.

It's there in the opening of the music that he describes. When the elders fall down in front of the lamb, each of them was holding two things: a harp, and a golden bowl of incense. John tells us what the incense is: it's the prayers of God's people, that is, of you and me. The heavenly scene is umbilically related to the earthly. The ordinary, faithful, humble prayers of Christians here on earth appear in heaven as glorious, sweet-smelling incense. I suspect the same is true of the music, with the heavenly harps corresponding to the song, however feeble and out of tune, which we sing to God's praise here and now. Then, in the first of the three songs in this passage, we find that the lamb is being praised, not just for rescuing us but for turning us from hopeless rebels into useful servants, from sin-slaves into 'a kingdom and priests'. From rubbish into royalty. This is our play. The lamb has set us free to stop being spectators and to start being actors.

We hear this crescendo of songs, then, not merely with excitement and eager fascination but with a sense of vocation. First, the praise of the lamb for what he's done (verses 9 and 10): he is indeed worthy to take and open the scroll and its seals. He is worthy (that is) to be the agent to carry forward God's plan to destroy the destroyers, to thwart the forces of evil, to confront the seemingly all-powerful and to establish his new order instead. And the way the lamb has done this is through his own death, his own blood. — Tom Wright, *Revelation for Everyone, For Everyone Bible Study*

*Guides* (London; Louisville, KY: SPCK; Westminster John Knox, 2011), 55–56.

## 13. What do we learn about Jesus from this passage?

And, if we are not either overwhelmed with the vision or exhausted with trying to understand it, we may glimpse here the most profound truth of all, which like everything else in chapters 4 and 5 continues to inform the whole of the rest of the book. The lamb shares the praise which belongs to the one and only God. This is John's own way of glimpsing and communicating the mind-challenging but central truth at the heart of Christian faith: Jesus, the lion-lamb, Israel's Messiah, the true man—this Jesus shares the worship which belongs, and uniquely and only belongs, to the one creator God.

But notice what this means. The affirmation of the full, unequivocal divinity of the lion-lamb comes, and only comes, in the context of the victory of God, through the lion-lamb, over all the powers of evil. It isn't enough just to agree with the idea, in the abstract, that Jesus is, in some sense or other, God. (People often say to me, 'Is Jesus God?', as though we knew who 'God' was ahead of time, and could simply fit Jesus in to that picture.) God, as we have already seen in Revelation, is the creator, who is intimately involved with his world, and worshipped by that world. God has plans and purposes to deliver his world from all that has spoiled it; in other words, to re-establish his sovereign rule, his 'kingdom', on earth as in heaven. It is at the heart of those plans, and only there, that we find the lion-lamb sharing the throne of the one God. The church has all too often split off a bare affirmation of Jesus' 'divinity' from an acceptance of God's kingdom-agenda. To do so is to miss the point, and to use a version of one part of the truth as a screen to stop oneself from having to face the full impact of the rest of the truth. We discover, and celebrate, the divinity of the lion-lamb Messiah only when we find ourselves caught up to share his work as the royal priesthood, summing up creation's praises before him but also bringing his rescuing rule to bear on the world. — Tom Wright, *Revelation for Everyone, For Everyone Bible Study Guides* (London; Louisville, KY: SPCK; Westminster John Knox, 2011), 58–59.

## 14. What do we learn about worship?

A number of words in the Bible are translated "worship." The one used the most often means "to bow down and do homage." Another biblical word for worship means "to kiss toward." Put the two words together, and you will have a good idea of what real worship is.

We worship God because He is worthy, bowing down in reverence and respect before Him. But we also "kiss toward" Him, which speaks of tenderness and intimacy.

We ought to be learning all we can about worship, because it will be one of the primary activities of heaven. And Jesus made it clear that there is a right and a wrong way to worship. There is true and false worship.

The Pharisees, who considered themselves the worship gurus of their day, missed the target by a mile. Jesus said of them, "'These people draw near to Me with their mouth, and honor Me with their lips, but their heart is far from Me. And in vain they worship Me, teaching as doctrines the commandments of men'" (Matthew 15:8-9).

Some people are too flippant and casual with God. They seem to think of Him as their celestial Big Buddy and approach Him that way in prayer: "Hey, Lord, how are You doing?" We need to be careful about that. In the Old Testament, God once said to a group of distracted and careless worshipers: "'A son honors his father, and a servant his master. If I am a father, where is the honor due me? If I am a master, where is the respect due me?' says the Lord Almighty" (Malachi 1:6, NIV).

Still others may recognize God as holy and all-powerful and may even tremble before Him, but they don't realize that God wants to be known in an intimate and personal way.

Yes, we are to revere and honor God. But we're also to embrace Him in closeness. We are to engage our hearts, with no hypocrisy. And that's where true worship begins.
— Greg Laurie, *Daily Hope for Hurting Hearts: A Devotional* (Dana Point, CA: Kerygma Publishing—Allen David Books, 2011).

## 15. Imagine you were there in this worship service for an hour. How do you think you would come back changed?

The word "worship" comes from the old English "worth-ship," which means to ascribe worth or value to something or someone. We should worship that which is worthy. A god of our own making is not worthy of worship.

I remember reading the story of Hideyoshi, a Japanese warlord who ruled over Japan in the late 1500s. He commissioned a colossal statue of Buddha for a shrine in Kyoto. It took fifty thousand men five years to build. The work had scarcely been completed when the earthquake of 1596 brought the roof of the shrine crashing down, wrecking the statue. In a rage, Hideyoshi shot an arrow at the fallen colossus, angry that he had worked so hard and the god could not even protect himself or his temple.

So it is with the gods we create for ourselves. Not so with God.

The Bible tells us about a choir in heaven joyfully singing of the "worth-ship" of Christ: "And they sang in a mighty chorus: 'The Lamb is worthy—the Lamb who was killed. He is worthy to receive power and riches and wisdom and strength and honor and glory and blessing'" (Revelation 5:12).

Jesus gave a great overview of the purpose of worship in his conversation with a woman at the well, recorded in John 4. At that time, the woman was lonely and miserable. She was thirsting for more than the water at the bottom of the well. In the course of their discussion, the woman turned the topic to places of worship. Jesus set the record straight, saying, "But the time is coming and is already here when true worshipers will worship the Father in spirit and in truth. The Father is looking for anyone who will worship him that way" (John 4:23). With these words, Jesus indicated the fundamental elements of true worship—worshiping "in spirit and in truth." — Greg Laurie, *New Believer's Guide to Effective Christian Living* (Carol Stream, IL: Tyndale House Publishers, Inc., 2002), 83–85.

## 16. What do we learn about angels?

No precise count is given in Scripture, but there's plenty of evidence that they make up a mighty multitude. In Revelation 5:11, John says he saw "ten thousand times ten thousand, and thousands of thousands" of angels around the throne. To give you a perspective on how many angels this is, the average football stadium in America holds about 50,000 people. It would take some 2,000 stadiums of that size to hold 100,000,000 people. The total number of angels John saw may have far exceeded 100,000,000 —10,000 was the highest numerical figure used in the Greek language. "Ten thousand times ten thousand" may have been John's way of describing an inexpressibly large company of angels.

In fact, Hebrews 12:22 says, "You have come to Mount Zion and to the city of the living God, the heavenly Jerusalem, to an innumerable company of angels," indicating that the population of angels is so large that they cannot be numbered. — David Jeremiah, *Answers to Your Questions about Heaven* (Carol Stream, IL: Tyndale, 2015).

## 17. What is the application of this passage? What difference does it make?

Now, this angelic vision is precisely the vision that possesses the thought life of the renovated heart; and you can see how it would grip the whole person and his or her earthly environment. This is what it is to "hallow" God's name. It is what we pray for in The Lord's Prayer. But, sad to say, even our Christian meetings and environments are for the most part far from it.

A. W. Tozer continues the passage quoted at length above as follows: "It is my opinion that the Christian conception of God current in these middle years of the twentieth century is so decadent as to be utterly beneath the dignity of the Most High God and actually to constitute for professed believers something amounting to a moral calamity."

But why a moral calamity? Because absolutely nothing can inform, guide, and sustain radical and radiant goodness in the human being other than this true vision of God and the worship based thereon. Only this vision can jerk the twisted condition of humanity right. Immanuel Kant said, "Nothing straight can be constructed from such warped wood as that which man is made of." And humanly speaking he was right. But what is impossible with men is possible with God. — Dallas Willard, *Renovation of the Heart: Putting on the Character of Christ* (Colorado Springs, CO: NavPress, 2002), 108.

## 18. Many see Jesus as a good moral teacher, but they do not see Him, as He is portrayed here as divine. What do you think of this view?

On the one side clear, definite moral teaching. On the other, claims which, if not true, are those of a megalomaniac, compared with whom Hitler was the most sane and humble of men. There is no half-way house and there is no parallel in other religions. If you had gone to Buddha and asked him "Are you the son of Bramah?" he would have said, "My son, you are still in the vale of illusion." If you had gone to Socrates and asked, "Are you Zeus?" he would have laughed at you. If you had gone to Mohammed and asked, "Are you Allah?" he would first have rent his clothes and then cut your head off. If you had asked Confucius, "Are you Heaven?" I think he would have probably replied, "Remarks which are not in accordance with nature are in bad taste." The idea of a great moral teacher saying what Christ said is out of the question. In my opinion, the only person who can say that sort of thing is either God or a complete lunatic suffering from that form of delusion which undermines the whole mind of man. If you think you are a poached egg, when you are looking for a piece of toast to suit you, you may be sane, but if you think you are God, there is no chance for you. We may note in passing that He was never regarded as a mere moral teacher. He did not produce that effect on any of the people who actually met Him. He produced mainly three effects—Hatred—Terror—Adoration. There was no trace of people expressing mild approval. — *God in the Dock*, "What Are We to Make of Jesus Christ?" (1950), para. 3, pp. 157–158. / Jerry Root and Wayne Martindale, *The Quotable Lewis* (Carol Stream, IL: Tyndale, 2010).

## 19. How important is the doctrine of the Deity of Christ? Can you be a Christian and not hold to the Deity of Christ?

Faith in the deity of Christ is necessary to being a Christian. It is an essential part of the New Testament gospel of Christ. Yet in every century the church has been forced to deal with people who claim to be Christians while denying or distorting the deity of Christ.

In church history there have been four centuries in which confession of the deity of Christ has been a crucial and stormy issue inside the church. Those centuries have been the fourth, fifth, nineteenth, and twentieth. Since we are living in one of the centuries where heresy assaults the church, it is urgent that we safeguard the church's confession of Christ's deity.

At the Council of Nicea in A.D. 325, the church, in opposition to the Arian heresy, declared that Jesus is begotten, not made, and that His divine nature is of the same essence (homo ousios) with the Father. This affirmation declared that the Second Person of the Trinity is one in essence with God the Father. That is, the "being" of Christ is the being of God. He is not merely similar to Deity, but He is Deity.

The confession of the deity of Christ is drawn from the manifold witness of the New Testament. As the Logos Incarnate, Christ is revealed as being not only preexistent to creation, but eternal. He is said to be in the beginning with God and also that He is God (John 1:1-3). That He is with God demands a personal distinction within the Godhead. That He is God demands inclusion in the Godhead.

Elsewhere, the New Testament ascribes terms and titles to Jesus that are clearly titles of deity. God bestows the preeminent divine title of Lord upon Him (Philippians

2:9-11). As the Son of Man, Jesus claims to be Lord of the Sabbath (Mark 2:28) and to have authority to forgive sins (Mark 2:1-12). He is called the "Lord of glory" (James 2:1) and willingly receives worship, as when Thomas confesses, "My Lord and my God!" (John 20:28).

Paul declares that the fullness of the Godhead dwells in Christ bodily (Colossians 1:19) and that Jesus is higher than angels, a theme reiterated in the book of Hebrews. To worship an angel or any other creature, no matter how exalted, is to violate the biblical prohibition against idolatry. The I ams of John's Gospel also bear witness to the identification of Christ with Deity. — R. C. Sproul, *Essential Truths of the Christian Faith* (Wheaton, IL: Tyndale House, 1992).

## 20. Can you become a Christian and not believe in the Deity of Christ?

A pastor in New York urged an intellectual but dissipated man to become a Christian. The man replied, "I cannot believe in the inspiration of the Bible, in the deity of Christ, or in prayer." "Do you believe in your own sins?" asked the pastor. "Oh, yes," replied the honest soul; "there is no doubt about my being a sinner and sometimes I am in hell!" "Are you willing to bring your sins to Christ for forgiveness and let Him, whatever you think of Him, take your guilt?" "But," he said, "I cannot believe in the inspiration of the Bible, or in the deity of Christ, or in prayer." "Just now," persisted the wise pastor, "I am not asking you to believe these things. You know you are a sinner, and in sin there is a taste of hell. Now, I offer you Jesus Christ as your Savior from sin. Will you accept Him as such, and leave all questions that puzzle you for future solution?" The man went to his home, and that night he accepted the Christ he knew as his Savior, and came to the meeting the next night to tell the people the joy of forgiveness that was in his soul. After several days of testimony which led others to Christ, the pastor gently asked, "What do you think now of the deity of Christ?" "Such a Savior," he said, with great emotion, "must be divine; if He were not divine He could not have done what He has done for me!" — *AMG Bible Illustrations, Bible Illustrations Series* (Chattanooga: AMG Publishers, 2000).

**21. What do you want to recall from today's conversation?**

**22. How can we support one another in prayer this week?**

Praying is a learned skill that takes time, discipline, and work. Corporate prayer is shallow because private prayer is infrequent. Recognize that we all have room to grow in learning to pray to God together. Be gracious with one another. Yet learn to guide a small group's prayer time. Here are a few suggestions.

**1. Remind the group what they're doing.**

Asking, "We have about 15 minutes left, anybody have a prayer request?" will inevitably solicit shallow and circumstantial requests of the "daily bread" variety. The way you've framed the time has devalued its very significance. Take the opportunity to remind the group what prayer is. Instead of saying, "Any prayer requests?" ask, "Now as we move from studying God's Word to praising him through prayer, what are some things God's Word has revealed to us?" Remind the group that prayer is communicating with the God of the universe through the access purchased for us by the costly sacrifice of the Son and enabled by the indwelling Holy Spirit. We can reflect back to God praise, adoration, thanksgiving, confession, and petition in light of his revelation. We are approaching a holy God through the mediation of his beloved Son, in whom we have union and fellowship. Help the group be awed by what they will embark upon so that the oft-neglected aspects of small group prayer—praise, adoration, confession, and thanksgiving—will become natural responses to what God has revealed.

## 2. Let Scripture guide your prayers.

If your group has just concluded a spirited study of a passage of Philippians (or whatever book you're studying), keep your Bibles open and let Scripture guide your time of prayer. God's revealed Word provides the content and trajectory for our prayers. Pray the commands from the passage you just studied, asking God to help you obey. Praise God for truths revealed in the passage, thanking him for who he is and how his power, wisdom, and majesty are revealed. Let the Scriptures guide how you pray. If you group has discerned the "big idea" from the passage, pray for those revealed truths to transform you, your small group, church, community, and world. If you've glimpsed an aspect of God's character, thank God for revealing it to you and praise him for his unchanging character. Ask for God's name to be hallowed in your life, in your community, and among the foreign peoples where your church missionaries are ministering.

Tim Keller, in his book Prayer: Experiencing Intimacy and Awe with God, describes Martin Luther's method of meditating upon a passage by discerning the instruction of the text (what does the text demand of me?) and then turning it into thanksgiving (how does this truth lead me to praise or thank God?), confession (how does this truth lead me to confess and repent?) and petition (how does this truth prompt me to appeal to God?). Providing your group a simple grid to move from the study of God's Word to praying God's Word will broaden the content of your prayers.

### 3. Get to the heart of the issue.

Many of us do not naturally discern what we really need. But Scripture opens our eyes to see our true needs in light of God's holiness, power, grace, and love. Perhaps someone shares a prayer request about being busy at work. This requires more information to know how to pray. To pray for more hours in a day or for this person to magically become more efficient is not likely to happen. Ask a few questions to better discern how to pray for this person. Is he busy because of a demanding and overbearing boss? If so, how can he live out his role as a God-honoring employee and make wise decisions on talking with his boss or prioritizing his workload? Is his busyness merely a symptom of an unhealthy desire to succeed, please others, or make the most money possible? Does he idolize his own success and the admiration he receives from others? Does he need to grow in contentment, gratefulness, and joy?

God cares about our "daily bread" requests, but he's also interested in exerting his kingdom and will in our hearts and minds. God is conforming us to his image from the inside out. So for Sally's cat Freckles, you can pray not merely for the health of the cat, but more importantly, for Sally's fear, anxiety, and loneliness that are being revealed.

### 4. Let Scripture evaluate your prayers.

Scripture is the best judge of our prayers. Do we generally communicate with God in various types of prayer (adoration, confession, thanksgiving, and supplication) or do we typically just list off our requests? Do we begin by praising God for his character and asking for his name to be hallowed as the Lord's Prayer instructs? Furthermore,

Scripture helps us discern why some of our prayers are actually unbiblical. Praying for a new Lexus to show up on your doorstep probably doesn't pass muster for being "daily bread." Keller writes, "One way petitionary prayer can actually do us harm is if we see it as a means to say to God, 'My will be done.' We are prone to indulge our appetites, telling God in no uncertain terms how he should run the universe. Such prayer neither pleases God nor helps us grow in grace." Does your small group just repeat and rephrase the request—"I pray for healing for Nancy's cancer"—or do you apply the gospel of Christ to the situation? Pray for healing from cancer, but also pray for joy and trust in Christ, confidence in her eternal destiny, patience with nurses and doctors, opportunity to encourage and witness to others, and ultimately that God would be glorified through this trial. http://www.thegospelcoalition.org/article/4-suggestions-to-deepen-your-small-group-prayer

# Revelation, Lesson #5
## Good Questions Have Small Groups Talking
### www.joshhunt.com

It is always good when the group can come together informed. But, in the case of this study of Revelation—and especially this week—it is really important. We dive neck deep into one of the visions of Revelation. Plead with your people to come as informed as they can. If they can read the notes from a study Bible, it would be great. If you have some readers who would read this section from a commentary, all the better. There are some free online commentaries here http://www.biblestudytools.com/commentaries/

## Revelation 9

## OPEN

Let's each share your name and one thing you are grateful for.

## DIG

**1. Overview. Read for emotion. What kind affect does John intend for his readers?**

It is already dark outside, and the wind is getting stronger. You are getting up to close the curtains when all the lights go out: a power failure. As you stumble your way to the cupboard by the back door in search of candles, you sense a cold wind coming at your face: the door is open! What's going on? Then you hear it: a low, growling, grinding sound, not far away. Grabbing a candle, you strike a match. The wind blows it out, but not before you catch a glimpse of Something just outside the door. Like a large dog, but … another match, you get the candle lit, but you wish you hadn't. It isn't a dog. It's—you don't know what it is. It's a monster! It's getting bigger! It's got huge teeth, enormous black wings, a long, spiky tail! You try to slam the door, but it's too late …

The stuff of horror movies, or nightmares, or both. We can only assume, when John wrote down this vision of the locusts, that he was intending to produce a similar effect. — Tom Wright, *Revelation for Everyone, For Everyone Bible Study Guides* (London; Louisville, KY: SPCK; Westminster John Knox, 2011), 85.

## 2. What would you say is the main point of this chapter?

God's judgment is painful and terrifying, and only those whom God seals will be protected from his judgment. — James M. Hamilton Jr., *Preaching the Word: Revelation—The Spirit Speaks to the Churches*, ed. R. Kent Hughes (Wheaton, IL: Crossway, 2012), 210.

## 3. Verse 1. Who do you think this fallen star is?

The first "terror" occurred when the fifth angel blew his trumpet. John saw a star that had fallen to earth from the sky. There is much debate as to the identity of this star, whether the "star" is Satan, a fallen angel, Christ, or a good angel. Some scholars point to 9:11 and identify this angel with the "angel from the bottomless pit," thus, a demon (see also 12:4, 9; Isaiah 14:12; Luke 10:18). If the star is a demon, he loosed evil forces upon the inhabitants of the earth. The evil forces, however, were only allowed to harm those who belonged to them, not the sealed believers (9:4). Most likely, this "star" is a good angel, because he was given the key to the shaft of the bottomless pit, and that key, normally, would be held by Christ (1:18), and because in 20:1 an angel came down from heaven with this key. If it is a good angel, then he was simply obeying God's directions to let loose calamity upon the earth. Most importantly, this angel is under God's control and authority. — Bruce Barton et al., *Life Application New Testament Commentary* (Wheaton, IL: Tyndale, 2001), 1230–1231.

## 4. Verse 1. What is the Abyss?

The bottomless pit, is the eternal destination of the wicked and the abode of the demonic forces (see Luke 8:31; 2 Peter 2:4; Jude 1:6; also referred to in 9:11; 11:7; 17:8; 20:1–3). It is full of smoke and fire, for when it was opened, smoke poured out as though from a huge furnace. There is so much smoke upon the opening of this pit that the sunlight and air were darkened. — Bruce Barton et al., *Life Application New Testament Commentary* (Wheaton, IL: Tyndale, 2001), 1231.

## 5. Can you think of other places in the Bible where locusts are mentioned?

Out of the billowing smoke come locusts. God had also sent a plague of locusts on Egypt (Exodus 10:1–20). This locust plague, however, fulfilled the words of the prophet Joel, who described a locust plague as a foreshadowing God's coming judgment (Joel 1:6–2:11). In the Old Testament, locusts symbolized destruction because they destroyed all vegetation (Deuteronomy 28:42; 1 Kings 8:37; Psalm 78:46). In what is called a plague, millions of locusts (grasshoppers) travel in a column many feet deep and miles in length. So many destroy everything in an area—grass, trees, and crops. This locust infestation spells destruction on agricultural societies. In the 1950s, locusts devoured several hundred thousand square miles of vegetation in the Middle East.

— Bruce Barton et al., *Life Application New Testament Commentary* (Wheaton, IL: Tyndale, 2001), 1231.

## 6. What do these locusts look like?

Someday Satan will be given the key to open the bottomless pit, a place where fallen spirits have been confined. With a burst of smoke, an army of powerful creatures will be released to the earth. Many people believe these are just some imaginary symbols placed in the Bible to startle or frighten us. I believe they will be as hideous as they are described.

The gruesome scenario begins when the bottomless pit is opened and a swarm of locusts emerge "like the smoke of a great furnace." The creatures are commanded to torture everyone who does not have the "seal of God" on his or her forehead. These hideous tormenters will be a terrifying bunch; they will look like horses, have faces like men, hair like women, and teeth like lions. The sound of their wings will be like chariots with many horses racing into battle (see Rev. 9:1–11). — David Jeremiah and Carole C. Carlson, *Invasion of Other Gods: The Seduction of New Age Spirituality* (Dallas: Word, 1995), 77.

## 7. Are these real locusts?

The difficulty of consistent literalism. Some instances of literalism seem to me strange, unreasonable, and unnecessary. For example, Robert Thomas holds that the eerie locusts of Revelation 9 and the strange frogs of Revelation 16 are demons who literally take on those peculiar physical forms, that the two prophets of Revelation 11 literally spew fire from their mouths, that every mountain in the world will be abolished during the seventh bowl judgments, that the fiery destruction of the literal city of Babylon will smolder for more than 1000 years, that Christ will return from heaven to earth on a literal horse, and that the new Jerusalem is literally a 1500-mile-high cube. — Kenneth L. Gentry Jr., "A Preterist View of Revelation," in *Four Views on the Book of Revelation*, ed. Stanley N. Gundry and C. Marvin Pate, Zondervan Counterpoints Collection (Grand Rapids, MI: Zondervan, 1998), 40.

### 8. What is unusual about these locusts?

Here, however, these locusts were told not to hurt the grass or plants or trees. This is a very different kind of "locust" plague, for they looked like horses (9:7; Joel 2:4) and they were given power to sting like scorpions. These "locusts" were terrifying. In fact, they were demons—evil spirits ruled by Satan who tempt people to sin. They did not attack vegetation but, instead, attacked all the people who did not have the seal of God on their foreheads (7:3). This invasion of demons tortured people who did not believe in God. Believers, however, were protected from this (3:10; 7:3–4). The demons were not allowed to kill people but to cause agony like the pain of scorpion stings. These would be so painful that people will seek death, but would be unable to do so. God would not allow them to escape punishment by dying—instead, they would have to suffer. The demons could only torment people for five months—the lifespan of a locust, as well as the length of the harvesttime on earth during which locusts plagues could come. The limitations placed on the demons show that they are under God's authority. — Bruce Barton et al., *Life Application New Testament Commentary* (Wheaton, IL: Tyndale, 2001), 1231.

### 9. Look carefully at verses 3, 4. What do we learn about Satan from this verse?

It's equally as important to comprehend that Satan and his army of fallen angels and even those who align themselves with the powers of darkness are locked into the bottomless pit of hell and are only permitted to venture from there when God allows them. Satan does not have the rule of this earth. Even though he and the other fallen angels are "principalities, … powers,… rulers of the darkness of this world" (Ephesians 6:12), they are not the rulers of the Kingdom of God on earth or in heaven which, through Jesus Christ, was made new. Demonic forces can only bind us if we subject ourselves to the places of darkness through sin and disobedience to God. Other than that, Satan and all other rebels of God are chained in darkness, impotent to touch the children of Light!

Before Jesus bowed His head on the cross and gave up the ghost, He said, "It is finished" (John 19:30). He could have meant His earthly ministry, and most likely did. But the depth of that statement may very well include the defeat and utter abolition of unrighteousness from the new order of the kingdom of God that Jesus came to establish on the earth. Jesus "spoiled principalities and powers, he made a shew of them openly, triumphing over them" (Colossians 2:15). Does that sound like there is more to do? Does that indicate that Jesus has to conquer them again here in Revelation? Of course not! Jesus did it on the Cross. Let's stop giving Satan the rule in areas in which he has been defeated. Any power that we see unleashed in Revelation is given by God only for a season and for a judgmental purpose. It is to that end that the fifth trumpet attack on mankind must be viewed. — Lerry W. Fogle, *Revelation Explained* (South Plainfield, NJ: Bridge Publishing, 1981), 195–196.

## 10. Job 1.8 – 11 is a good cross-reference. Someone read that passage for us. What do we learn about Satan from this passage?

Satan is on a leash and he is only free on earth to the length of his chain. He cannot go beyond God's permission. But if we don't enforce his judgment in our own lives, we will be victims instead of victors. — David Jeremiah, *Sanctuary: Finding Moments of Refuge in the Presence of God* (Nashville, TN: Integrity Publishers, 2002), 177.

## 11. What else do you recall that the Bible teaches about Satan?

It's been often noted that when people think about Satan, they tend toward extremes. Throughout church history, two serious distortions about the person and power of Satan have persisted. The first is to deny his reality or to fail to take him seriously as a potent spiritual adversary. The second distortion is to attribute greater power and authority to him than he actually possesses, as if God and Satan were equal combatants, fighting it out to the finish, vying for supremacy. Nothing could be further from the truth. The battle between God and Satan is no contest. God is all-powerful, or omnipotent; Satan is not. It's that clear-cut. Satan is a created being and is in no way equal to God. Not even close. This is proved by at least seven points.

1) Satan could not dethrone God in his rebellion. When he rebelled, God expelled him from His presence.

2) Apparently, all the angels, fallen and unfallen, regularly reported to God (Job 1:6; 2:1). This demonstrates God's authority over Satan and his angels.

3) God places clear limits and restraints on Satan in Job 1–2. Satan could not afflict Job without God's

permission, and God limited the extent of the suffering Satan could inflict upon him.

4) Satan could not successfully tempt Jesus into sinning (Matthew 4:1-11).

5) Satan will not be able to defeat God in the end (Revelation 19:11-21).

6) Satan will be bound for 1000 years in the abyss (Revelation 20:1-3).

7) Satan will be punished by God forever in the lake of fire (Revelation 20:10).

Robert Lightner says it well:

> Satan must never be viewed as God's equal, vying with God for control of the world. God and Satan are not similar to the good side and dark side of the "force" portrayed in Star Wars...God and Satan are not in a cosmic struggle to gain control of the world, for God alone is in control and sovereign. Satan is like a dog on his master's leash. He cannot do anything anywhere, anytime, to anybody, without God's permission. Yes, he is God's enemy and ours, but he is an enemy who must obey God even though he hates Him.

Erwin Lutzer agrees.

> The devil is just as much God's servant in his rebellion as he was God's servant in the days of his sweet obedience. Even today, he cannot act without God's express permission; he can neither tempt, coerce, demonize, nor make so much as a single plan without the consent and approval of God.

As Martin Luther famously said, "The devil is God's devil."

To summarize the limitations on Satan's power and influence, "He is powerful, but not omnipotent. He is smart but not omniscient. He can travel the universe, but he is not omnipresent." — Mark Hitchcock, *101 Answers to Questions about Satan, Demons, and Spiritual Warfare* (Eugene, OR: Harvest House, 2014).

## 12. How powerful is Satan? To what degree should we fear Satan?

Christ called Peter knowing every flaw in him. He gave that flawed apostle a new assignment and a new name to go with it and, by heaven, the call would be accomplished even if Christ had to do it Himself. I believe Jesus loved Peter's passion, but His cherished disciple also had some ingredients that could prove less palatable to the call. I'd like to suggest that everything standing between Simon the fisherman and Peter the Rock needed to go.

Satan had a sieve. Christ had a purpose. The two collided. Satan got used. Peter got sifted. "Simon, Simon, Satan has asked to sift you as wheat." For reasons only our wise, trustworthy God knows, the most effective and long-lasting way He could get the Simon out of Peter was a sifting by Satan. He was right. You see, the One who called us is faithful, and He will do whatever it takes to sanctify us to fulfill our callings. Yes, it's that important. Remember, there are huge things going on out there that we just don't understand.

To me, the sifting of Peter can easily and with sound theology be compared to a full-scale attack by Satan on those with wholehearted, sincere, and pure devotion to Christ. In some ways, Peter's situation was in a league of its own considering he was the backbone of the brand-new Hebrew-Christian church. On the other hand, Christ loves all of us with everything in Him. No, we're not among those first disciples, but you and I have been called to be disciples or followers of Christ in our own generations. He is just as watchful and protective over us.

I believe God allows Satan a certain amount of leash where believers are concerned, but I am convinced that if he wants more than his daily allowance, he has to get permission. None of us is of less importance to Christ than Peter, John, or the apostle Paul. He would never take lightly one of Satan's attacks on His followers. For Satan to launch a full-scale attack of seduction on a wholehearted, sincere, and purely devoted follower of Christ, you bet I believe he has to get permission. — Beth Moore, *When Godly People Do Ungodly Things: Finding Authentic Restoration in the Age of Seduction* (Nashville: B&H, 2002).

## 13. Should Christians study Satan?

C. S. Lewis said in his introduction to The Screwtape Letters that we're often guilty of two equal and opposite errors. One is to disbelieve in the existence of Satan. The other is an excessive, unhealthy obsession with him. With either, he is delighted. We need to realize the danger of each of these. If one doesn't believe in the reality of a personal devil and the spiritual powers of darkness that exist in our world, that makes one extremely vulnerable. Not only does it deny the truth of God's Word, but such skepticism gives Satan free reign to influence our thoughts and behavior. But on the other hand, to have an excessive, unhealthy obsession with Satan—the attitude that the devil made me do it or there is a demon behind every bush—attributes to him a power and control that he just does not have. Giving the enemy excessive attention feeds his deceptive lies, and deception and brings our thoughts and attitudes into conformity with his perspective. Rather, in faith we must believe the truth of God's Word and accept that the victory God has given us is reality. — Jerry Rankin and Beth Moore, *Spiritual Warfare* (Nashville: B&H, 2009).

## 14. What are some common misunderstandings about Satan?

We also make a mistake in how we think of Satan relative to the Holy Spirit, especially in our understanding of the battle between the flesh and the spirit. We often consider them on a par with each other, as if they were two equal combatants seeking to claim our allegiance and control our actions. There is a tension between good and evil; Satan seeks to entice us to choose his way while the Holy Spirit is jealous for us as God's possession. We are often deceived even in our distorted understanding of the warfare. Persuaded that Satan has a power that, in fact, he does not have, we readily give in to our selfish nature, an inclination to sin and embrace carnal, worldly values. That Satan has such a power is an illusion fed by his deception.

Who is the Holy Spirit that lives within us? He is Almighty God—Jesus Christ, to whom all power and authority have been given. But who is Satan? The devil is a created being, a fallen angel. The word angel in the Scripture means "messenger." While angels are spiritual, heavenly hosts created to worship God, their assigned role is that of a messenger. As a messenger, Satan primarily speaks to our minds. There are Old Testament passages that speak of disasters and affliction being attributed to Satan. Jesus spoke of the woman bent over as being in bondage to Satan, but Satan does not have power in the physical realm except as it is granted by God. If Satan were given authority and power over the physical domain of life, expressways would be a massive pileup of wrecks, and everybody would be stricken with cancer. But he doesn't have that kind of power or liberty to destroy life. As in the example of Job, he was able to do nothing apart from God's permission, and the only reason God allowed him physically to afflict Job was so that God would be ultimately glorified. God is sovereign over the universe, and Satan is only a messenger, a fallen angel. His only power and authority are in speaking to our minds, hence his strategy is to deceive us that we might embrace something that is not true and contrary to God's Word. — Jerry Rankin and Beth Moore, *Spiritual Warfare* (Nashville: B&H, 2009).

## 15. What do we learn about God from this chapter?

The general meaning of these trumpets is clear. Throughout this entire period, extending from the first to the second coming, our exalted Lord Jesus Christ, who rules all things in accordance with the scroll of God's decree, will again and again punish the persecutors of the Church by inflicting upon them disasters in every sphere of life, both physical and spiritual. The blood of the martyrs is precious in the sight of the Lord. The prayers of all the saints are heard. God sees their tears and their suffering. Yet, in spite of all these warning voices, mankind in general does not repent. Foolish and stubborn men continue to transgress both the first (verse 20), and the second table of the law (verse 21). The persecuting world becomes the impenitent world. It is impenitence that brings about not only the outpouring of the bowls of final wrath (chapters 15, 16) but also the culmination of this wrath in the final judgment. Delay is now no longer possible. — William Hendriksen, *More than Conquerors: An Interpretation of the Book of Revelation* (Grand Rapids, MI: Baker Books, 1967), 123.

## 16. Notice the language in verse 15: this very hour and day and month and year. What is the lesson for us?

Let's not forget that their release will follow God's timetable. They cannot move their human puppet rulers to action until the exact moment God allows. Though they serve their master, Satan, they cannot act apart from the sovereign permission of God. In fact, God has planned their release for a specific "hour and day and month and year" (9:15). Never think that life is merely a series of haphazard events tossed into the air by blind fate for us mortals to catch or dodge! On the contrary, we can rest in the confidence that whatever comes our way is known not only by our all-knowing, omnipotent God, but it is directed by Him according to His good purposes. As we read in Romans 8:28, "We know that God causes all things to work together for good to those who love God, to those who are called according to His purpose." As we'll soon see, those things that work together for the good of God's elect do not always mean the good of everybody.

When the angels of death are released, they go out to kill a third of humanity (9:15). Verse 18 reveals that they will succeed. Don't run past this figure too quickly! A third of humanity today is over two billion people! Don't forget that by this time many people on earth have already suffered destruction in which a quarter of the earth's population had been decimated (6:8). No wonder God has actively restrained these wicked angels for so many centuries! Second Peter 3:9 declares, "The Lord is not slow about His promise, as some count slowness, but is patient toward you, not wishing for any to perish but for all to come to repentance." God's gracious disposition toward the world staves off the relentless wrath of the forces of evil, but when this present window of opportunity for repentance closes, a dark cloud of wrath will quickly close in. The several verses fill in the details of how this holocaust will be accomplished.
— Charles R. Swindoll, *Insights on Revelation, Swindoll's New Testament Insights* (Grand Rapids, MI: Zondervan, 2011), 141.

## 17. Look at verse 5. What do we learn about suffering from this verse?

But the purpose of such judgments is to turn people to repentance, so even this limitation may also serve to allow repentance (9:20–21). Five months' of torment (9:5), like 1,260 days of torment (cf. 11:10), thus contrasts with eternal torment (14:10–11; 20:10). That the locusts harm no vegetation but only people without God's seal (9:4) also turns the attentive listener back to 7:3, where vegetation should not be harmed until God had sealed his servants. This connection reinforces the point: God specifically exempts his servants from this judgment, perhaps emphasized especially if this is a demonic army. — Craig S. Keener, *Revelation, The NIV Application Commentary* (Grand Rapids, MI: Zondervan Publishing House, 1999), 269.

## 18. What is the application for us? What do we need to remember in times of suffering?

Right now, right where you are—remember, God has put a limit on all adversity. Because you are a child of God, Jesus Christ is living inside of you. He knows how much you can bear. We are capable of withstanding the pressure only because of our relationship to Jesus Christ. We can endure the suffering and hardship to the limit God has given. — Charles F. Stanley, *Dealing With Life's Pressures*, electronic ed. (Atlanta: In Touch Ministries, 1997).

## 19. Verses 20, 21. What was the goal of sending these locusts?

The locusts' mission, though, is not simply instant destruction. That would, it seems, be too kind. They are to torture people until they long to die but are unable to do so (verse 6).

As with the plagues of Egypt, so we must assume that the aim here is to challenge the inhabitants of the earth to repent. This point eventually emerges in verses 20 and 21, which function somewhat like the comments in Exodus about Pharaoh and his court: though they saw the plagues, they hardened their hearts, until eventually the writer declares that God himself had hardened their hearts, to make them all the more ready for the judgment when it finally came. — Tom Wright, *Revelation for Everyone, For Everyone Bible Study Guides* (London; Louisville, KY: SPCK; Westminster John Knox, 2011), 87.

## 20. Why do you think this chapter is in the Bible? What is the application? How does it change our thinking?

We have a great need to see evil for what it is. The sins that tempt us are not pleasant things that we could enjoy if it weren't for those pesky, unnecessary, burdensome commands that God has given to us. The sins that tempt us are traps set by a Dark Lord far more evil than Sauron, and his lieutenants are far more frightful than the Nazgûl. We need to feel the evil of sin, so that we will be convinced that God's commands are good. God's commands keep us from the traps and snares of the ancient dragon. We need to feel this, and we also need to be convinced that God will indeed judge sin. We need to be convinced that God alone can save. And we need to be convinced that idolatry and sin will not profit us. God gives us chapter 9 to meet these needs. — James M. Hamilton Jr., *Preaching the Word: Revelation—The Spirit Speaks to the Churches*, ed. R. Kent Hughes (Wheaton, IL: Crossway, 2012), 209–210.

## 21. How can we support one another in prayer this week?

One day, Rosalind was in a prayer group when she heard an older missionary praying about something she knew had already been taken care of, and so she prayed, "Lord, that prayer has already been answered!" Yes, that frank abruptness disturbed some of the old timers, but others quickly grasped the importance of complete sincerity in prayer. Out of this developed a concept that has helped millions of people. It is called "conversational prayer."

Here's how it works: two or more people form a prayer group based on the words of Jesus, "Again, I tell you that if two of you on earth agree about anything you ask for, it will be done for you by my Father in heaven. For where two or three come together in my name, there am I with them" (Matt. 18:19–20). Miss Rinker suggests that when you pray, use short simple phrases, talking to Jesus as though He were another person in your group. She has even suggested that you put an empty chair in your group, talking to Him as though He were actually sitting there.

She suggested that you begin with thanksgiving, focusing on several items for which you are thankful; but unlike formal prayer, the sentences are short. This kind of prayer is a dialogue—not a monologue where someone prays around the world for everything that he or she can think of. Then, after giving thanks, focus on praying for needs. — Harold J. Sala, *Touching God: 52 Guidelines for Personal Prayer* (Nashville: B&H, 2013).

It is always good when the group can come together informed. But, in the case of this study of Revelation—and especially this week—it is really important. We dive neck deep into one of the visions of Revelation. Plead with your people to come as informed as they can. If they can read the notes from a study Bible, it would be great. If you have some readers who would read this section from a commentary, all the better. There are some free online commentaries here http://www.biblestudytools.com/commentaries/

## Revelation 12

## OPEN
Let's each share your name and where were you born?

## DIG

1.  **We gotta know what the Bible says before we can understand what it means. Let's read it, then let me ask one (or several) of you to summarize what we have read.**

    These six verses contain the first symbolic picture. The scene is heaven. Here John sees a woman gloriously arrayed: the sun is her garment, the moon her footstool and a wreath of twelve stars her crown. This woman is about to give birth to a child. She cries because she is in labour. Suddenly John sees standing in front of the woman a fiery red dragon. Think of a winged serpent with crested head and destructive claws, cruel, savage, malignant, vicious; but remember that this is a picture, a symbol. Now this beast has seven crowned heads and ten horns. So immense in size is this dragon that its mammoth tail furiously lashing across the sky sweeps away one-third of the stars of heaven and flings them to earth! Why does this terrible monster stand in front of the woman who is about to give birth to a child? In order to devour her child as soon as it is born! Does the dragon succeed? He does not. The woman gives birth to a son, a male, a mighty one, who is to shepherd the heathen with an iron rod. Then suddenly ... but let us hear what happened in the apostle's own words: 'And snatched away was her child unto God and unto his throne.' Having failed in his attempt to devour the child, the dragon now directs all his fury against the radiant, all-glorious woman. But the woman flees into the wilderness where God has prepared food and shelter for her for 1,260 days. We shall read more later about the dragon's attempt to destroy the woman (see verse 13). — William Hendriksen, *More than Conquerors: An Interpretation of the Book of* Revelation (Grand Rapids, MI: Baker Books, 1967), 135.

2. **Overview. There are several schools of thought when it comes to Revelation. Futurist believe most of Revelation will happen in the future. The Preterist view holds that most what Revelation is what will soon take place (Revelation 1) — meaning, what will happen in the first century. In other words, most of is what is in Revelation has already happened. Does this story look like something that has already happened?**

This woman is in labour to bear a child who is undoubtedly the Messiah, Christ, compare Rev 12:5 where he is said to be destined to rule the nations with a rod of iron. That is a quotation from Ps 2:9 and was an accepted description of the Messiah. The woman, then, is the mother of the Messiah.

(i) If the woman is the "mother" of the Messiah, an obvious suggestion is that she should be identified with Mary; but she is so clearly a superhuman figure that she can hardly be identified with any single human being.

(ii) The persecution of the woman by the dragon suggests that she might be identified with the Christian Church. The objection is that the Christian Church could hardly be called the mother of the Messiah.

(iii) In the Old Testament the chosen people, the ideal Israel, the community of the people of God, is often called the Bride of God. "Your Maker is your husband" (Isa 54:5). It is Jeremiah's sad complaint that Israel has played the harlot in disloyalty to God (Jer 3:6-10). Hosea hears God say: "I will betroth you to me for ever" (Hos 2:19-20). In the Revelation itself we hear of the marriage feast of the Lamb and the Bride of the Lamb (Rev 19:7; Rev 21:9). "I betrothed you to Christ," writes Paul to the Corinthian Church, "to present you as a pure bride to her one husband" (2 Cor 11:2).

This will give us a line of approach. It was from the chosen people that Jesus Christ sprang in his human lineage. It is for the ideal community of the chosen ones of God that the woman stands. Out of that community Christ came and it was that community which underwent such terrible suffering at the hands of the hostile world. We may indeed call this the Church, if we remember that the Church is the community of God's people in every age.

From this picture we learn three great things about this community of God. First, it was out of it that Christ came; and out of it Christ has still to come for those who have never known him. Second, there are forces of evil, spiritual and human, which are set on the destruction of the community of God. Third, however strong the opposition against it and however sore its sufferings, the community of God is under the protection of God and, therefore, it can never be ultimately destroyed. — *Barclay's Daily Study Bible (NT)*.

### 3. What does this story have in common with the Christmas story?

Now occurs the final act in this mighty drama. The scene is Bethlehem. There in a manger lies the Christ-child. But although He is now actually born, the dragon still tries to destroy Him. In fact, Revelation 12, though covering with a few words the entire previous history of Satan's warfare against the Christ, refers directly and specifically to the events that took place in connection with Christ's birth. 'And the dragon stands in front of the woman who is about to be delivered, that when she is delivered he may devour her child.'

The wise men from the East are in the audience room of Herod. 'Be sure', says Herod, 'to report to me as soon as you shall have found the child, that I also may come and worship him.' His intention was to kill the child. But the wise men, warned of God, returned to their country another way after they had found and worshipped the Christ. Still the dragon refuses to admit defeat. The infants of Bethlehem and district, two years old and under, are slain. But Herod failed. So did the dragon. The Christ-child was safe in Egypt (Mt. 2:13). God's purpose can never be frustrated. Christ's birth in Bethlehem is God's victory over the dragon. The Saviour's death on the cross for His people is His further victory. 'And snatched away was her child to God and to His throne.' This refers to Christ's ascension and enthronement (Rev. 5:7; cf. Phil. 2:9). Those who oppose Him will be treated to 'the iron rod'. This is true throughout this entire dispensation. Christ triumphs and the angels sing 'Glory to God in the highest!' — William Hendriksen, *More than Conquerors: An Interpretation of the Book of Revelation* (Grand Rapids, MI: Baker Books, 1967), 140.

## 4. Assume this woman is a picture of God's bride—Old and New Testament saints. What does it mean that she was clothed with the sun?

The woman was "clothed with the sun" (2:1), an illustrative way of indicating she shone with the brightness of Jesus, the Light of the world. Indeed Jesus clothes the people of God with white raiment and the pure light of His righteousness. The moon was "under her feet," which indicates she was standing on the firm foundation of the Church, a reflection of the Sun (Jesus). The "lesser light" that rules the night, a term used for the moon, represents the Church, which has been granted all power and authority over spiritual darkness (night). Israel, the people of God, is standing on that firm foundation. The Church is victorious over any spiritual force that opposes God, even death. "And upon her head a crown of twelve stars" (2:1). This is a crown for our Lord Jesus, the Head of the Church and the focus of Revelation. The twelve stars represent either the twelve tribes of Israel, the apostles of Christ or both. In any case, they characterize the government of God in Israel, the Church. — Lerry W. Fogle, *Revelation Explained* (South Plainfield, NJ: Bridge Publishing, 1981), 224–225.

## 5. What do we learn about ourselves from this?

There are three characters. First, there is the radiant woman. That woman symbolizes the Church (cf. Is. 50:1; 54:1; Ho. 2:1; Eph. 5:32). Scripture emphasizes the fact that the Church in both dispensations is one. It is one chosen people in Christ. It is one tent; one vineyard; one family—Abraham is the

father of all believers whether they are circumcised or not—
one olive tree; one elect race, royal priesthood, holy nation,
people for God's own possession; one beautiful bride; and
in its consummation one new Jerusalem whose gates bear
the names of the twelve tribes and whose foundations are
inscribed with the names of the twelve apostles. (Cf. Is. 54;
Am. 9:11; Mt. 21:33 ff.; Rom. 11:15–24; Gal. 3:9–16, 29; Eph.
2:11; 1 Pet. 2:9 (cf. Ex. 19:5, 6); Rev. 4:4; 21:12–14.)

On earth this Church may appear very insignificant
and open to scorn and ridicule; but from the aspect of
heaven this same Church is all-glorious: all that heaven
can contribute of glory and of splendour is lavished upon
her. She is clothed with the sun, for she is glorious and
exalted. She has the moon under her feet, for she exercises
dominion. She has on her head a wreath of twelve stars, for
she is victorious. She was pregnant, for it was her task to
bring forth the Christ 'as concerning the flesh' (Rom. 9:5). —
William Hendriksen, *More than Conquerors: An Interpretation
of the Book of Revelation* (Grand Rapids, MI: Baker Books,
1967), 135–136.

## 6. Who is the child?

There are three characters. First, there is the radiant woman.
That woman symbolizes the Church (cf. Is. 50:1; 54:1; Ho. 2:1;
Eph. 5:32). Scripture emphasizes the fact that the Church in
both dispensations is one. It is one chosen people in Christ.
It is one tent; one vineyard; one family—Abraham is the
father of all believers whether they are circumcised or not—
one olive tree; one elect race, royal priesthood, holy nation,
people for God's own possession; one beautiful bride; and
in its consummation one new Jerusalem whose gates bear
the names of the twelve tribes and whose foundations are
inscribed with the names of the twelve apostles. (Cf. Is. 54;

Am. 9:11; Mt. 21:33 ff.; Rom. 11:15–24; Gal. 3:9–16, 29; Eph. 2:11; 1 Pet. 2:9 (cf. Ex. 19:5, 6); Rev. 4:4; 21:12–14.)

On earth this Church may appear very insignificant and open to scorn and ridicule; but from the aspect of heaven this same Church is all-glorious: all that heaven can contribute of glory and of splendour is lavished upon her. She is clothed with the sun, for she is glorious and exalted. She has the moon under her feet, for she exercises dominion. She has on her head a wreath of twelve stars, for she is victorious. She was pregnant, for it was her task to bring forth the Christ 'as concerning the flesh' (Rom. 9:5). — William Hendriksen, *More than Conquerors: An Interpretation of the Book of Revelation* (Grand Rapids, MI: Baker Books, 1967), 135–136.

7. **Let's look at this from a different perspective. Someone look up Galatians 4.19. Think of the woman as God's people, past and present. Galatians 4.19 says that Christ is being formed in us. What do we learn about this process from this passage?**

"And she being with child cried, travailing in birth, and pained to be delivered" (12:2). The Romans were told that "the whole creation groaneth and travaileth in pain together until now" (Romans 8:22). In both texts, the idea is this: the people of God are suffering the birth pangs that come before delivery. They are having Christ formed within them. They are dying to self. They are decreasing that Jesus may increase. They are putting off the old man and putting on the new (Ephesians 4:22–24; Colossians 3:9–10). These things are as painful as the contractions of birth. They make the people of God cry out in pain. — Lerry W. Fogle, *Revelation Explained* (South Plainfield, NJ: Bridge Publishing, 1981), 225.

## 8. Who is the dragon?

Thirdly, there is the dragon. It symbolizes Satan (Rev. 20:2). The seven crowned heads indicate the devil's world-dominion (cf. Eph. 2:2; 6:12). See also our explanation of Revelation 13:1 and 17:9. These crowns, however, are not wreaths of victory but merely crowns of arrogated authority. The ten horns indicate Satan's destructive power; he stands in front of the woman in order to devour her child! When Satan fell, he dragged along with him in his ruin 'one-third of the stars of heaven', that is, a vast number of evil spirits (cf. Job 38:7; 2 Pet. 2:4; Jude 6). — William Hendriksen, *More than Conquerors: An Interpretation of the Book of Revelation* (Grand Rapids, MI: Baker Books, 1967), 136.

## 9. What does it mean that his tail swept a third of the stars out of the sky?

"His tail drew the third part of the stars of heaven, and did cast them to the earth" (12:4). This is another way of saying that there were many angels who also fell with the rebellion of Satan (or Lucifer). He rejected the authority of God and, in the process, influenced a sector of the heavenly populace. All of these were cast down from the heavenly realm. Jude 6 supports this amply. — Lerry W. Fogle, *Revelation Explained* (South Plainfield, NJ: Bridge Publishing, 1981), 226.

## 10. What is the main teaching of this chapter?

Let us now study the main thought. It is this—the dragon stands in front of the woman who is about to be delivered so that when she is delivered he may devour her child; that is, Satan is constantly aiming at the destruction of the Christ. Thus viewed, the entire Old Testament becomes one story, the story of the conflict between the seed of the woman and the dragon, between Christ and Satan. In this conflict Christ is, of course, victorious. — William Hendriksen, *More than Conquerors: An Interpretation of the Book of Revelation* (Grand Rapids, MI: Baker Books, 1967), 136–137.

## 11. Verse 5. The child being snatched up to God... what does that refer to? When was Jesus snatched up to God?

The child which the woman bore was destined to rule the nations with a rod of iron. As we have seen, this quotation from Ps 2:9 indicates that the child was the Messiah.

When the child was born, he was rescued from the dragon by being snatched up to heaven, even to the throne of God. The word used here for the child being snatched up is the same as is used in 1 Th 4:17 to describe the Christian being caught up to meet the Lord in the air (compare 2 Cor 12:2 where Paul uses it to tell of himself being caught up into the third heaven).

In a sense this is a puzzling passage. As we have seen, the reference is to Jesus Christ as Messiah, and, as John tells it, the story goes straight from his Birth to his Ascension; the snatching up must refer to the Ascension. As the Acts has it: "He was lifted up" (Ac 1:9). The strange thing is the total omission of the earthly life of Jesus. This is due to two things.

It is due to the fact that John is not at the moment interested in anything other than the fact that Jesus Christ was delivered by the direct action of God from the hostile powers which continually attacked him.

It is due also to the fact that all through the Revelation John's interest is not in the human Jesus but in the exalted Christ, who is able to rescue his people in the time of their distresses. — *Barclay's Daily Study Bible (NT)*.

## 12. Verse 6. What is the wilderness?

The wilderness represents a place of spiritual refuge and protection from Satan, probably not meant to be literal because this chapter is mostly symbolic. John the Baptist had lived in the wilderness before beginning his public ministry (Luke 1:80; 3:2). After he had been tempted by Satan in the wilderness, Jesus had been ministered to by the angels (Mark 1:13). Jesus had withdrawn to the wilderness with his disciples before returning to Jerusalem the last time (John 11:54). After the apostle Paul had been converted, he had gone away "into Arabia" (most likely, into the wilderness, Galatians 1:17) before returning to begin his ministry. Thus, in this verse, the woman fleeing into the wilderness is a picture of her escaping to a place of protection.

In this place prepared by God, he cared for her for 1,260 days—the same number noted for the trampling of the holy city (11:2), the ministry of the two witnesses (11:3), and the rule of the Beast (13:5). God would care for his people during the entire time when evil would be in control in the world. In the wilderness, God's people would be hounded by the people on the earth (those who would follow the Beast), but God would watch over them. Many would be martyred, but God would care for them. The word translated "care for" is literally "nourish." The woman will be provided with food miraculously, just as Elijah was cared for in the wilderness by God (1 Kings 17:2–4). God also provided manna in the wilderness for his people (Exodus 16:4). — Bruce B. Barton, *Revelation, ed. Grant R. Osborne, Life Application Bible Commentary* (Wheaton, IL: Tyndale House Publishers, 2000), 139.

## 13. What is the lesson for us of this wilderness?

Some think that this woman pictures the Jewish believers only. Others suggest that she symbolizes all believers, the true Israel. Depending on one's view of when the believers will be taken to heaven (before, in the middle of, or after this time of Great Tribulation), these symbols may be identified in different ways. Because God has chosen not to make it clear, it is best to simply understand that God is promising spiritual protection for his people who are still on the earth during this difficult time. — Bruce B. Barton, *Revelation, ed. Grant R. Osborne, Life Application Bible Commentary* (Wheaton, IL: Tyndale House Publishers, 2000), 140.

## 14. What do we learn about God from this passage?

Because God aided the woman's escape into the desert, we can be sure that he offers security to all true believers. Satan always attacks God's people, but God keeps them spiritually secure. Some will experience physical harm, but all will be protected from spiritual harm. God will not let Satan take the souls of God's true followers. When Satan's attacks seem overpowering, remember that God is ruler over all. Trust him. — Bruce B. Barton, *Revelation, ed. Grant R. Osborne, Life Application Bible Commentary* (Wheaton, IL: Tyndale House Publishers, 2000), 140.

## 15. What do we learn about Christian living?

Does it sometimes seem to you that Satan has the upper hand in the struggle of the ages? Does it look like he is the one who knows how to fight to win, and God always seems to pick the losing strategy? Turn the other cheek. Bless those who persecute you. Love your enemies. Preach Christ and him crucified and not with what the world thinks is eloquent wisdom. Choose the weak things of the world. It's almost as though God shows up on the playground to pick his team, and instead of picking the guys who look like they can play, he picks the obviously inferior team. And how does it always turn out? God triumphs every time.

Do you ever look around your life and feel like God has dealt you a losing hand? If you're a student of the Bible, when you see what looks like a losing hand, you know that God is about to triumph in a way that will give him all the credit for the victory. Isn't that the kind of victory you want? So when everything in your life looks unimpressive, sure to lose, insignificant, trust Christ and watch for the glory of God to be demonstrated.

When you feel like a loser, when you feel like a failure, when you feel like you're incompetent, praise God! You're exactly the kind of person God uses. God uses people like us to defeat the great dragon.

This is precisely what happens when the child is caught up to God and to his throne in 12:5. In verse 4 the dragon is poised to devour the child. God looks like he has the short end of the stick. Satan is a dragon, and God has left this poor pregnant woman and her newborn baby to face the dragon alone. Suddenly victory is snatched from the dragon's jaws as the child is caught up to God and his throne.

This being caught up to Heaven seems to collapse the whole life of Jesus, from ministry to cross and resurrection, so that we go straight from the birth to the ascension. When Jesus died on the cross, it looked like Satan had conquered. But God turned certain and total defeat—his own people rejecting and crucifying the Messiah—into the victory that saves the world. When it looked like the last defense against evil had fallen, Christ rose from the dead, decisively breaking the back of evil.

Do you know this victory? Do you believe that God turns loss into gain? Do you believe that God has irrevocably defeated Satan through the death of Jesus on the cross? Faith comes by hearing, and hearing by the word of Christ (Romans 10:17). Believe it. — James M. Hamilton Jr.,

*Preaching the Word: Revelation—The Spirit Speaks to the Churches,* ed. R. Kent Hughes (Wheaton, IL: Crossway, 2012), 248–249.

## 16. What do we learn about Satan from verse 10?

Can't you see him? Pacing back and forth before God's bench. Can't you hear him? Calling your name, listing your faults.

He rails: "This one you call your child, God. He is not worthy. Greed lingers within. When he speaks, he thinks often of himself. He'll go days without an honest prayer. Why, even this morning he chose to sleep rather than spend time with you. I accuse him of laziness, egotism, worry, distrust..."

As he speaks, you hang your head. You have no defense. His charges are fair. "I plead guilty, your honor," you mumble.

"The sentence?" Satan asks.

"The wages of sin is death," explains the judge, "but in this case the death has already occurred. For this one died with Christ."

Satan is suddenly silent. And you are suddenly jubilant. You realize that Satan cannot accuse you. No one can accuse you! Fingers may point and voices may demand, but the charges glance off like arrows hitting a shield. No more dirty dishwater. No more penance. No more nagging sisters. You have stood before the judge and heard him declare, "Not guilty."

"The Lord GOD helps me, so I will not be ashamed. I will be determined, and I know I will not be disgraced. He shows that I am innocent, and he is close to me. So who can accuse me? If there is someone, let us go to court together" (Isa. 50:7–8).

Once the judge has released you, you need not fear the court. — Max Lucado, *In the Grip of Grace* (Dallas, TX: Word Pub., 1996), 177–178.

## 17. Do you ever feel accused? What are we to do when we feel accused?

Day after day, hour after hour. Relentless, tireless. The Accuser makes a career out of accusing. Unlike the conviction of the Holy Spirit, Satan's condemnation brings no repentance or resolve, just regret. He has one aim: "to steal, and to kill, and to destroy" (John 10:10). Steal your peace, kill your dreams, and destroy your future. He has deputized a horde of silver-tongued demons to help him. He enlists people to peddle his poison. Friends dredge up your past. Preachers proclaim all guilt and no grace. And parents, oh, your parents. They own a travel agency that specializes in guilt trips. They distribute it twenty-four hours a day. Long into adulthood you still hear their voices: "Why can't you grow up?" "When are you going to make me proud?"

Condemnation—the preferred commodity of Satan. He will repeat the adulterous woman scenario as often as you permit him to do so, marching you through the city streets and dragging your name through the mud. He pushes you into the center of the crowd and megaphones your sin:

This person was caught in the act of

immorality . . . stupidity . . . dishonesty . . . irresponsibility.

But he will not have the last word. Jesus has acted on your behalf.

He stooped. Low enough to sleep in a manger, work in a carpentry shop, sleep in a fishing boat. Low enough to rub shoulders with crooks and lepers. Low enough to be spat upon, slapped, nailed, and speared. Low. Low enough to be buried.

And then he stood. Up from the slab of death. Upright in Joseph's tomb and right in Satan's face. Tall. High. He stood up for the woman and silenced her accusers, and he does the same for you.

He "is in the presence of God at this very moment sticking up for us" (Rom. 8:34 MSG). Let this sink in for a moment. In the presence of God, in defiance of Satan, Jesus Christ rises to your defense. He takes on the role of a priest. "Since we have a great priest over God's house, let us come near to God with a sincere heart and a sure faith, because we have been made free from a guilty conscience" (Heb. 10:21–22 NCV).

A clean conscience. A clean record. A clean heart. Free from accusation. Free from condemnation. Not just for our past mistakes but also for our future ones.

"Since he will live forever, he will always be there to remind God that he has paid for [our] sins with his blood" (Heb. 7:25 TLB). Christ offers unending intercession on your behalf.

Jesus trumps the devil's guilt with words of grace. — Max Lucado, *Shaped by Grace: You Are God's Masterpiece in the Making* (Nashville: Thomas Nelson, 2012).

## 18. What is the difference between Satan's accusing and the Holy Spirit's convicting?

You would think that Satan, having led the person into sin, would then leave him to suffer the consequences; but this is not what happens. He wants to make the disobedient Christian doubly defeated. It's his "double whammy!"

When you and I have disobeyed God, Satan moves in for that finishing stroke. Satan still uses this tactic with great effect! "You call yourself a Christian? Do you think a holy God will hear your prayer! Ha! After what you did?"

See how subtle he is? Before we sin, while he is tempting us, he whispers "You can get away with this…" After we sin he shouts "You will never get away with this… ."

It is very, very important that we learn to distinguish between Satan's accusation and the Spirit's conviction. A feeling of guilt and shame isn't necessarily a bad thing if it comes from the Spirit of God. But if it drives us to despair and hopelessness, we've listened to the wrong voice.

When the Spirit of God convicts you, He uses the Word of God in love and seeks to bring you back into fellowship with your heavenly Father. When Satan accuses you he uses your own sins in a hateful way, and seeks to make you feel helpless and hopeless.

Remember his End Game. "To steal, to kill, and to destroy"! Satan wants you to feel guilty and condemned. He wants you to experience regret and remorse—but not repentance. He wants to keep accusing you so that you focus your attention on yourself and your sins…and let your eyes slip away from the Lord who loves you and redeems you. In contrast, true conviction from the Spirit will move you closer to the Lord. — Greg Laurie, *10 Things You Should Know about God and Life* (Dana Point, CA: Kerygma Publishing—Allen David Books, 2011).

## 19. What do we learn about the devil and how to defeat him from this passage?

"Your adversary, the devil," puts it well. That's the way Peter identifies the Enemy—boldly, without equivocation.

"The devil" comes from the word diabolos, which means "slanderer" or "accuser." Revelation 12:10 states that the enemy of our souls is "the accuser of our brethren." He accuses us "day and night," according to that verse. Not only does he accuse us to God, he also accuses us to ourselves. Many of our self-defeating thoughts come from the demonic realm. He is constantly accusing, constantly building guilt, constantly prompting shame, constantly coming against us with hopes of destroying us.

Did you notice his style? "He prowls about." The Devil is a prowler. Think about that. He comes by stealth, and he works in secret. His plans are shadowy. He never calls attention to his approach or to his attack. Furthermore, he is "like a roaring lion." He is a beast, howling and growling with hunger, "seeking someone to devour"! To personalize this, substitute your name for "someone." When you do, it makes that verse all the more powerful. "Your adversary, the devil, prowls about like a roaring lion, seeking to devour _____." I find that has a chilling effect on my nervous system.

He isn't simply out to tantalize or to tease us. He's not playing around. He has a devouring, voracious appetite. And he dances with glee when he destroys lives, especially the lives of Christians.

A. T. Robertson wrote, "The devil's purpose is the ruin of mankind. Satan wants all of us." It's wise for us to remember that when we travel. It's wise for us to remember that when we don't gather for worship on a Sunday and we're really out on our own. It's wise to remember that when we find ourselves alone for extended periods of time, especially during our more vulnerable moments. He prowls about, stalking our every step, waiting for a strategic moment to catch us off guard. His goal? To devour us . . . to consume us . . . to eat us alive.

I hope you've gotten a true picture of your enemy. He's no sly-looking imp with horns, a red epidermis, and a pitchfork. He is the godless, relentless, brutal, yet brilliant adversary of our souls who lives to bring us down . . . to watch us fall.
— Charles R. Swindoll, *Laugh Again & Hope Again* (Nashville: Thomas Nelson, 2009).

## 20. How can we support one another in prayer this week?

# Revelation, Lesson #7
## Good Questions Have Small Groups Talking
### www.joshhunt.com

Email your group and ask them to do a little reading on Heaven. There is an excellent chapter in a book I co-authored with Brandon Park called *After Life*. It is a short read, but coves all the highlights.

## Revelation 21

## OPEN
Let's each share your name and one thing you look forward to about Heaven

## DIG

1. **Verse 1. I wonder how much the new earth will be like this earth. What do you think? What might be the same? What will be different?**

   The first heaven and the first earth have passed away. In our imagination let us try to see this new universe. The very foundations of the earth have been subjected to the purifying fire. Every stain of sin, every scar of wrong, every trace of death, has been removed. Out of the great conflagration a new universe has been born. The word used in the original implies that it was a 'new' but not an 'other' world. It is the same heaven and earth, but gloriously rejuvenated, with no weeds, thorns or thistles, and so on. Nature comes into its own; all of its potentialities, dormant so long, are now fully realized. The 'old' order has vanished. The universe in which the dragon, the beast, the false prophet, and the harlot were carrying out their programme of iniquity has vanished. — William Hendriksen, *More than Conquerors: An Interpretation of the Book of Revelation* (Grand Rapids, MI: Baker Books, 1967), 198–199.

## 2. Why do you suppose there won't be any more sea?

The sea, as we now know it, is no more. At present the sea is the emblem of unrest and conflict. The roaring, raging, agitated, tempest-tossed waters, the waves perpetually engaged in combat with one another, symbolize the nations of the world in their conflict and unrest (13:1; 17:15). It is the sea out of which the beast rises. But in the renewed universe—the new heaven and earth—all will be peace. The heaven and the earth and the sea as they now are shall vanish. The universe is going to be gloriously rejuvenated and transformed. 'And the city, the holy one, new Jerusalem, I saw coming down out of the heaven from God, having been made ready as a bride adorned for her husband.' — William Hendriksen, *More than Conquerors: An Interpretation of the Book of Revelation* (Grand Rapids, MI: Baker Books, 1967), 199.

## 3. Why does there need to be a new Heaven?

Due to the pollution and destruction of our planet, we understand the need for a new earth. But what is the reason for a new heaven? According to Job 15:15, the heavens are not clean in God's sight. Why? Because Satan's presence has polluted them (Revelation 12:10). — Jon Courson, *Jon Courson's Application Commentary* (Nashville, TN: Thomas Nelson, 2003), 1788.

4. **Verse 3. What is the most important thing we need to know about Heaven?**

But the most important thing about the city is that God dwells there with His people. The Bible gives an interesting record of the dwelling places of God. First, God walked with man in the Garden of Eden. Then He dwelt with Israel in the tabernacle and later the temple. When Israel sinned, God had to depart from those dwellings. Later, Jesus Christ came to earth and "tabernacled" among us (John 1:14). Today, God does not live in man-made temples (Acts 7:48-50), but in the bodies of His people (1 Cor. 6:19-20) and in the church (Eph. 2:21-22). — *The Bible Exposition Commentary – New Testament, Volume 2.*

5. **Let me rapid fire some questions about Heaven. First, what do you think we will look like in Heaven?**

The Bible doesn't answer all our questions about Heaven. However, this question is put to rest—at least in part—in 1 John 3:2: "What we will be has not yet been made known. But we know that when he appears, we shall be like him, for we shall see him as he is."

It is only natural to be curious about what we do not know. We long to know what is over the hill. Many have searched the Scriptures for a hint of what our bodies will look like in the afterlife.

What we'll look like in Heaven isn't stated in the Bible, but it seems that we will recognize one another, just as Moses and Elijah were recognized by the disciples who were witnesses of Jesus' transfiguration (Matthew 17:1–8). The Bible says "for the LORD does not see as man sees; for man looks at the outward appearance, but the LORD looks at the heart" (1 Samuel 16:7 NKJV). Part of Heaven's glory is that our bodies will be transformed, and we will become like Jesus Christ in His perfect resurrected body. We won't be subject to the ills and ravages of old age like we are now, for we will be changed.

Only God could take two eyes, a nose, and a mouth, and make every person who has ever lived an individual—totally unique. It's not inconceivable, then, that God in Heaven can perfect His children—who bear His image—without changing their individual uniqueness.

While the Bible doesn't say exactly what we'll look like, it does tell us that our faces will reflect the face of our Redeemer. "[We] will see Your face in righteousness; [we] shall be satisfied when [we] awake in Your likeness" (Psalm 17:15 NKJV). Heaven will not reflect our earthly desires; instead we will reflect Heaven's King, our Lord Jesus Christ. — Billy Graham, *The Heaven Answer Book* (Nashville: Thomas Nelson, 2012).

## 6. What will we do in Heaven?

Science fiction writer Isaac Asimov said, "I don't believe in an afterlife, so I don't have to spend my whole life fearing hell, or fearing heaven even more. For whatever the tortures of hell, I think the boredom of heaven would be even worse."

Sadly, even among Christians, it's a prevalent myth that Heaven will be boring. Sometimes we can't envision anything beyond strumming a harp and polishing streets of gold. We've succumbed to Satan's strategies "to blaspheme God, and to slander his name and his dwelling place" (Revelation 13:6).

People sometimes say, "I'd rather be having a good time in Hell than be bored out of my mind in Heaven." Many imagine Hell as a place where they'll hang around and shoot pool and joke with friends. That could happen on the New Earth, but not in Hell.

Hell is a place of torment and isolation, where friendship and good times don't exist. Hell will be deathly boring. Everything good, enjoyable, refreshing, fascinating, and interesting originates with God. Without God, there's nothing interesting to do. David wrote, "In Your presence is fullness of joy; at Your right hand are pleasures forevermore" (Psalm 16:11, NKJV). Conversely, outside of God's presence, there is no joy.

Our belief that Heaven will be boring betrays a heresy—that God is boring. There's no greater nonsense. What's true is that our desire for pleasure and the experience of joy come directly from God's hand. God designed and gave us our taste buds, adrenaline, sex drives, and the nerve endings that convey pleasure to our brains. Likewise, our imaginations and our capacity for joy and exhilaration were made by the very God we accuse of being boring! Do we imagine that we ourselves came up with the idea of fun?

"Won't it be boring to be good all the time?" Note the underlying assumption: Sin is exciting, righteousness is boring. We've fallen for the devil's lie. His most basic strategy, the same one he employed with Adam and Eve, is to make us believe that sin brings ful-fillment. But the opposite is true. Sin robs us of fulfillment. Sin doesn't make life interesting; it makes life empty. Sin doesn't create adventure; it blunts it. Sin doesn't expand life; it shrinks it. Sin's emptiness inevitably leads to boredom. When there's fulfillment, when there's beauty, when we see God as he truly is—an endless reservoir of fascination—boredom becomes impossible.

Those who believe there can't be excitement without sin think with sin-poisoned minds. Drug addicts are convinced that without their drugs they can't live happy lives. In fact—as every one else can see—drugs make them miserable. Freedom from sin will mean freedom to be what God intended, freedom to find far greater joy in everything. In Heaven we'll be filled, as Psalm 16:11 describes it, with joy and eternal pleasures.

Another reason why people assume Heaven is boring is that their Christian lives are boring. That's not God's fault. He calls us to follow him in an adventure that should put us on life's edge. If we're experiencing the invigorating stirrings of God's Spirit, trusting him to fill our lives with divine appointments, and experiencing the childlike delights of his gracious daily kindnesses, then we'll know that God is exciting and Heaven is exhilarating. What else could they be?

As for having nothing to do in Heaven, we're going to help God run the universe (Luke 19:11-27). We'll have an eternity full of things to do. The Bible's picture of resurrected people at work in a vibrant society on a resurrected earth couldn't be more compelling. (No wonder Satan works so hard to rob us of it.)

God will give us renewed minds and marvelously constructed bodies, full of energy and vision. James Campbell says, "The work on the other side, whatever be its character, will be adapted to each one's special aptitude and powers. It will be the work he can do best; the work that will give the fullest play to all that is within him." Even under the Curse, we catch glimpses of how work can be enriching, how it can build relationships, and how it can help us to improve ourselves and our world. Work stretches us in ways that make us smarter, wiser, and more fulfilled.

The God who created us to do good works (Ephesians 2:10) will not abandon this purpose when he resurrects us to inhabit the new universe.

We are told that we will serve God in Heaven (Revelation 7:15; 22:3). Service is active, not passive. It involves fulfilling responsibilities, in which we expend energy. Work in Heaven won't be frustrating or fruitless; it will involve lasting accomplishments, unhindered by decay and fatigue, and enhanced by unlimited resources. We'll approach our work in Heaven with the same enthusiasm we now bring to our favorite sports or hobbies.

In Heaven, we'll reign with Christ, exercise leadership and authority, and make important decisions. This implies specific delegated responsibilities for those under our leadership, as well as specific responsibilities given to us by our leaders (Luke 19:17-19). We'll set goals, devise plans, and share ideas. Our best workday on Earth—when everything turns out better than we planned, when we get everything done on time, when everyone on the team pulls together and enjoys each other—is just a small foretaste of the joy our work will bring us on the New Earth. — Randy Alcorn, *50 Days of Heaven: Reflections That Bring Eternity to Light* (Carol Stream, IL: Tyndale, 2006).

### 7. Will we be confined to one place, or will we be able to travel in Heaven?

To say that we will be "confined" to Heaven would indicate that there is something more . . . something still missing. The Bible's promise to us is that Jesus will be there to welcome us into His inexpressible splendor and we will be satisfied. If we are satisfied, then we will not want anything more (Psalm 17:15). "I have placed before you an open door that no one can shut" (Revelation 3:8). Heaven's gates will never be shut (Revelation 21:25). Jesus said, "It is your Father's good pleasure to give you the kingdom" (Luke 12:32 NKJV).

We would have a small faith if we believed that God's work among His people would be diminished in Heaven compared to what He did among us on earth. "Can you search out the deep things of God? Can you find out the limits of the Almighty? They are higher than heaven" (Job 11:7 NKJV). The Bible speaks of "heaven and the heaven of heavens [that] cannot contain God" (1 Kings 8:27 NKJV). The psalmist said, "Such knowledge is too wonderful for me. . . . I cannot attain it" (Psalm 139:6 NKJV). When we get to Heaven, we will be in His presence forever. Jesus said, "Where I am, there you may be also" (John 14:3 NKJV). Our earthly minds are limited, but when we move to God's country, our understanding will be illuminated. We will not want to leave because His glory will take eternity to explore.

In Heaven, our knowledge will be perfect—and so will all creation. "Creation itself will be liberated from its bondage to decay and brought into the glorious freedom of the children of God" (Romans 8:21). Will we ride on chariots of clouds or walk on the wings of the wind like the Lord? (Psalm 104:3).

We don't know the scope of our activity in Heaven, but Jesus promised that we would be with Him. Stop and consider this wondrous God. — Billy Graham, *The Heaven Answer Book* (Nashville: Thomas Nelson, 2012).

## 8. Will we see people in Heaven we couldn't get along with on earth?

We'll not only see them, but we'll get along with them perfectly. In Heaven, the past will be forgiven; they will be perfect—and so will we!

God's forgiveness means the complete blotting out of the dirt and degradation of our past, present, and future. This is our hope in Christ—that we are made new through Him. That process begins when we surrender our lives to Jesus Christ (2 Corinthians 5:17)—and it will be perfected in Heaven. "You have come to . . . the city of the living God.

... to the spirits of righteous men made perfect" (Hebrews 12:22–23).

An unforgiving spirit holds a grudge against someone who has offended us. Some people just naturally rub us the wrong way, just as we rub some people the wrong way. But how will we feel when we meet them in Heaven? Paul reminds us that in a flash, we will be changed (1 Corinthians 15:51–55).

In the meantime, it's impossible to be at peace with ourselves and with others if we have an unforgiving heart, which is a sin. The Bible says, "Everyone who has this hope in [Christ] purifies himself, just as [Christ] is pure" (1 John 3:3).

Guilt and unforgiving feelings are the focal point of much psychiatric counseling. So tremendous is the weight of our guilt that the great and glorious truth of God's forgiveness should encourage every believer in Jesus Christ. God's goodness in forgiving us means even more when we realize that—through faith in Christ—we are without guilt in God's sight; we are clothed forever with Christ's righteousness. The only reason our sins can be forgiven is because Jesus Christ paid their full penalty on the cross.

The Bible tells us that a sinful mind is hostile to God (Romans 8:7), but in Heaven we will have total peace (Luke 19:38). We will be completely changed when we get to Heaven—and so, too, will those we couldn't get along with while on earth.

If God can make the lion and the lamb lie down together, we can trust Him to take care of our fractured relationships as we enter our heavenly home. — Billy Graham, *The Heaven Answer Book* (Nashville: Thomas Nelson, 2012).

## 9. Will we grieve for lost loved ones when we are in Heaven?

In God's glorious presence, all our concerns and griefs will be erased.

It's hard to imagine how we can be happy if our loved ones aren't in Heaven because of their unbelief, but Scripture assures that "even the memory of them will disappear" (Psalm 9:6 TLB). God's plan will be revealed, in all of its fullness, in Heaven. Our present understanding is limited, but one day we will comprehend the perfection of His justice and mercy: "The former things will not be remembered, nor will they come to mind. . . . be glad and rejoice" (Isaiah 65:17–18).

The human mind has but a wisp of understanding. As believers, through the work of the Holy Spirit, our faith grows deeper concerning the things of God. He first gives us faith to believe in Him, then our faith and knowledge of His Word grow so we understand that He can and will do all things well. He demonstrated this by giving His life as a ransom for many (Mark 10:45).

Paul says, "Now I know in part; then I shall know fully, even as I am fully known. And now these three remain: faith, hope, and love. But the greatest of these is love" (1 Corinthians 13:12–13). We must have these three gifts from God to live for Him on earth. In Heaven, our faith will be complete, for we will see Him face-to-face. In Heaven, our hope will become reality, for we will no longer have to patiently endure before being fully in His presence. And the love that He exhibited for us on earth and instilled in us to love Him and others will continue forever, because God is love (1 John 4:8).

The scope of God's love will not be fully realized until it is revealed in Heaven. The mystery of God's love would not be a mystery if we knew all the answers. All our concern, worry, and grief will come to an end when we begin new life in Heaven. — Billy Graham, *The Heaven Answer Book* (Nashville: Thomas Nelson, 2012).

## 10. Will we be judged in Heaven or receive rewards in Heaven?

At the judgment seat of Christ, believers will receive rewards—not the reward of eternal life, for that has already been given to them, but of other blessings God has for us.

The apostle Paul compared this to an athletic contest in which the victor would appear before a judge who would determine his reward, not his punishment. We can understand this when we think of the Olympics. Athletes compete for a prize. Some receive bronze medals; others, silver; and first-place winners receive the gold. This is the thought behind the judgment seat in Heaven.

Believers will not be judged for their sin, for Christ dealt with our sin on the cross at Calvary. Instead, at the judgment seat, our work on earth for Christ's Kingdom will be evaluated and rewarded according to God's perfect righteousness and justice.

The fact that we can stand before Him at all is a miracle of His grace in our lives. Then, what we do in obedience and by the strength of the Holy Spirit will be evaluated, and "each will be rewarded according to his own labor. For we are God's fellow workers; you are God's field, God's building" (1 Corinthians 3:8–9). This is a tremendous incentive to work for the Lord, with the right motive in our hearts. We won't all receive the same rewards. We do not have the same abilities, but we will be judged according to our faithful response to the gifts and opportunities given to us.

And it's not just the work of reaching out to those in need of the gospel, but also how we conduct ourselves in body and mind (2 Peter 3:11). God's rewards are incentives for us to live a holy life of faithful service to Christ—not to others—during our time on earth. These rewards are described as crowns, as we see in Paul's letter to Timothy: "I have fought the good fight. . . . There is laid up for me the crown of righteousness, which the Lord, the righteous Judge, will give to me on that Day, and not to me only but also to all who have loved His appearing" (2 Timothy 4:7–8 NKJV).

Jesus said, "Rejoice and be glad, because great is your reward in heaven" (Matthew 5:12). Then He gave us a remarkable promise: "Behold, I am coming soon! My reward is with me, and I will give to everyone according to what he has done" (Revelation 22:12). The greatest reward of all will be to hear our Lord saying, "Well done, good and faithful servant!" (Matthew 25:23). — Billy Graham, *The Heaven Answer Book* (Nashville: Thomas Nelson, 2012).

## 11. Do people who have died and gone to Heaven know what is going on down here on earth?

Heaven will be glorious. We will meet the saints of old. There we will walk the streets of gold and be reunited with those we love. When we enter Heaven, we will have crossed the finish line to meet the One who will reveal stories yet untold.

Consider the scene in Hebrews 12:1 describing the heroes of the faith who are now in Heaven: "Since we are surrounded by such a great cloud of witnesses . . . let us run with perseverance the race marked out for us." While we aren't given any detail, the previous chapter in Hebrews gives us examples of that "great cloud of witnesses"—the

121

saints of old who ran the race of faith and finished well. We draw strength from their victorious finish on earth, bearing testimony to their faith in God and God's faithfulness to them.

Absolutely nothing can be hidden from Him. The Bible does not tell us if the souls in God's presence know what is happening on earth. What it does tell us is that God knows what is happening in our lives. Our desire as believers should not be to please men (Galatians 1:10), but to run the race to please God: "My eyes are fixed on you, [O LORD]" (Psalm 141:8). And Jesus Christ watches our every move and knows our every thought. How thankful we should be, for He is our strength: "The eyes of the LORD range throughout the earth to strengthen those whose hearts are fully committed to him" (2 Chronicles 16:9).

Do we welcome the eyes of the Lord? Do we live each day knowing that the Lord of Heaven looks down on us? He is not waiting for us to stumble, but He is there when we do. He is seeking our loyalty to Him: "Whatever you do, work at it with all your heart, as working for the Lord, not for men, since you know that you will receive an inheritance from the Lord as a reward. It is the Lord Christ you are serving" (Colossians 3:23–24). — Billy Graham, *The Heaven Answer Book* (Nashville: Thomas Nelson, 2012).

## 12. Can we be sure we will go to heaven?

Do you know for certain that you have eternal life and that you will go to Heaven when you die? God wants you to be sure! The Bible says: "I write these things to you who believe in the name of the Son of God so that you may know that you have eternal life" (1 John 5:13). Suppose you were standing before God right now and He asked you, "Why should I let you into Heaven?" What would you say? You may not know what to reply. What you need to know is that God loves us and has provided a way that we can know for sure where we will spend eternity. The Bible states it this way: "For God so loved the world that He gave His only Son, that whoever believes in Him shall not perish but have eternal life" (John 3:16).

We have to first understand the problem that is keeping us from Heaven. The problem is this - our sinful nature keeps us from having a relationship with God. We are sinners by nature and by choice. "For all have sinned and fall short of the glory of God" (Romans 3:23). We cannot save ourselves. "For by grace are you saved, through faith, and this not of yourselves – it is the gift of God. Not by works, so that no one can boast" (Ephesians 2:8-9). We deserve death and hell. "For the wages of sin is death" (Romans 6:23).

God is holy and just and must punish sin, yet He loves us and has provided forgiveness for our sin. Jesus said: "I am the way and the truth and the life. No one comes to the Father except through me" (John 14:6). Jesus died for us on the cross: "For Christ died for sins once for all, the righteous for the unrighteous to bring you to God" (1 Peter 3:18). Jesus was resurrected from the dead: "He was delivered over to death for our sins and was raised to life for our justification" (Romans 4:25).

So, back to the original question – "How can I know for sure that I will go to Heaven when I die?" The answer is this – believe in the Lord Jesus Christ and you will be saved (Acts 16:31). "To all who received Him, to those who believed in His Name, He gave the right to become children of God" (John 1:12). You can receive eternal life as a FREE gift. "The gift of God is eternal life in Christ Jesus our Lord" (Romans 6:23). You can live a full and meaningful life right now. Jesus said: "I have come that they may have life, and have it to the full" (John 10:10). You can spend eternity with Jesus in

Heaven, for He promised: "And if I go and prepare a place for you, I will come back and take you to be with me that you may also be where I am" (John 14:3).

If you want to accept Jesus Christ as your Savior and receive forgiveness from God, here is prayer you can pray. Saying this prayer or any other prayer will not save you. It is only trusting in Jesus Christ that can provide forgiveness of sins. This prayer is simply a way to express to God your faith in Him and thank Him for providing for your forgiveness. "God, I know that I have sinned against You and am deserving of punishment. But Jesus Christ took the punishment that I deserve so that through faith in Him I could be forgiven. I place my trust in You for salvation. Thank You for Your wonderful grace and forgiveness! Amen!" Read more: http://www.gotquestions.org/know-sure-Heaven.html#ixzz3TcY1jGst

### 13. How good do we have to be to get into Heaven?

The answer may shock you—but the truth is that we will never be good enough to go to Heaven on our own.

Why is this? The reason is because God is absolutely pure and holy, and no evil can ever enter His home. Just one sin will keep us away from His presence—and no one can claim to be sinless. We are born in sin (Romans 5:12); we are sinners by nature. The Bible says, "For all have sinned and fall short of the glory of God" (Romans 3:23).

God doesn't take our good deeds and bad deeds and weigh them against each other; if He did, He'd be letting us into Heaven with our sins. God's standard is nothing less than perfection. We may think we're good enough—but if so, we are filled with pride, which is a sin. The Bible says, "If we claim to be without sin, we deceive ourselves and the truth is not in us" (1 John 1:8). But Jesus preached repentance to receive eternal life in Heaven (Mark 1:15), and it is through His shed blood that our sins are forgiven, covered by His goodness, and this is why those who believe in Him will be received into Heaven.

Suppose you had a barrel of water and it had been filtered and distilled until no impurities remained. If someone asked you to drink it, you wouldn't hesitate. But suppose someone put a drop of raw sewage in it. Would you drink it? Of course not. The same is true with sin.

This is why God sent His Son, the Lord Jesus Christ, to earth to redeem us by His love and His sacrifice. Jesus was without sin because He was God in human flesh—but on the cross all our sins were transferred to Him, and He took the judgment we deserve.

Don't trust in yourself and your good works, but turn to Jesus and trust Him alone for your salvation. It is the life-changing decision that will settle once and for all your place in Heaven. Don't miss what the Lord has in store for those who love Him and are willing to let Him be the Master of their lives. — Billy Graham, *The Heaven Answer Book* (Nashville: Thomas Nelson, 2012).

## 14. How did Jesus' death make it possible for us to go to Heaven?

By His death Jesus paid the penalty for our sins. This alone gives us everlasting life with Him in Heaven.

We are so used to sin that we easily forget just how serious it is in the eyes of God. Every sin we commit is an act of rebellion—a deliberate renunciation of God's rightful authority over us. But sin is serious for another reason: it ravages our souls, bringing heartache and brokenness into our lives. Most of all, it cuts us off from fellowship with God.

Because of God's great love for us, however, He provided the way for us to be forgiven and cleansed of our sins—and, ultimately, to spend eternity with Him. We could never cleanse ourselves; sin's stain is too deep. But God made our forgiveness possible by sending Jesus Christ into the world as the final and complete sacrifice for our sins. On the cross, Jesus took the divine judgment that you and I deserve. He died in our place. The Bible says, "For Christ died for sins once for all, the righteous for the unrighteous, to bring you to God" (1 Peter 3:18).

Do you want freedom from sin's penalty? Believe that Christ died for you. He suffered for you. He won the battle over sin for you. He rose from the grave and was victorious over death so that you can live forever. But you must respond by receiving Him into your heart by faith and by committing your life to Him without reserve. He is waiting for you to confess your sins, to surrender yourself to Him, and to make Him Lord and Master of your life. He is preparing a place in Heaven for all those who will come to Him in faith and complete submission. Don't delay. Make sure of your salvation by turning your life over to Him now. — Billy Graham, *The Heaven Answer Book* (Nashville: Thomas Nelson, 2012).

## 15. Will people who claim to believe in Jesus and yet never show any signs of a changed life go to Heaven when they die?

Only God knows people's hearts, and whether or not they honestly gave their life to Christ.

Jesus warned, however, that "not everyone who says to me, 'Lord, Lord,' shall enter the kingdom of heaven, but only he who does the will of my Father who is in heaven" (Matthew 7:21). No Christian is perfect, of course—but someday our true relationship with Christ will be revealed. The Bible warns, "Everything is uncovered and laid bare before the eyes of him to whom we must give account" (Hebrews 4:13).

Nevertheless, one of the signs of a true Christian is a changed life. In fact, if there is no indication that a person wants to follow Christ, it strongly suggests that their faith may not be sincere and they may not be saved. The Bible compares a person like this to a corpse—physically present but lifeless (James 2:26). This is a sobering truth.

We must not deceive ourselves into thinking that we will be saved if we haven't truly trusted Christ as Savior and aren't seeking to follow Him as Lord. "By their fruit you will recognize them" (Matthew 7:20). One day Christ will acknowledge to His Father in Heaven those who belong to Him and have demonstrated the fruit of His Spirit.

Are you seeking to follow Christ in every area of your life—with His help? It is the only way to live victoriously. — Billy Graham, *The Heaven Answer Book* (Nashville: Thomas Nelson, 2012).

## 16. Can you repent for the first time just before you die and still go to Heaven?

One of the Bible's greatest truths is that God stands ready to forgive us whenever we turn to Him in repentance and faith—even at the end of life. The Lord wants all people to come to repentance. The Bible says, "He is patient with you, not wanting anyone to perish, but everyone to come to repentance" (2 Peter 3:9).

The Bible repeatedly warns us, however, not to wait until the last minute. For one thing, we do not know what the future holds; life is uncertain. Death can snatch us from this world in an instant, before we could even cry out to God. If a person is dying of a heart attack and, out of fear, prays for

God's salvation, is that repentance sincere? Only the Lord knows. My question for such a person would be this: If you didn't want anything to do with Christ while you were living, why would you want to spend eternity with Him?

But we do find an answer in Scripture for someone who is sincere of heart. When Jesus was hanging on the cross between two criminals, one mocked Jesus because He wouldn't save Himself. But the other turned to Jesus and, in faith, cried out, "Jesus, remember me when you come into your kingdom." Christ replied, "I tell you the truth, today you will be with me in paradise" (Luke 23:42–43). Although he had only a brief time to live, he received the gift of salvation.

The Bible says, "I tell you, now is the time of God's favor, now is the day of salvation" (2 Corinthians 6:2). Don't presume upon God's grace. Don't treat lightly Christ's death on the cross. Don't risk being flat on your back and looking up toward Heaven before answering the most important question that confronts you: What will you do with Jesus? Receive Him today. — Billy Graham, *The Heaven Answer Book* (Nashville: Thomas Nelson, 2012).

## 17. Will there be animals in Heaven?

The Bible tells us that animals were a very important part of God's creation. "God made all sorts of wild animals, livestock, and small animals, each able to produce offspring of the same kind. And God saw that it was good" (Genesis 1:25).

The Bible also says, "The LORD God formed from the ground all the wild animals and all the birds of the sky. He brought them to the man to see what he would call them, and the man chose a name for each one" (Genesis 2:19). Only humans and animals were formed from the earth, which makes us special. Now, let's get it straight: Animals weren't created in God's image, and they aren't equal to humans in any way. But still, God created animals and cares about them, which means we should care about them too.

People and animals share something unique: We're living beings. The fact that God has a future plan for people and for the earth strongly suggests that he has a future plan for animals as well.

Some kids who have been bitten or hurt by animals are afraid of them—but on the New Earth, no animals will be dangerous, and we'll never be afraid. We'll love being around them, just like Adam and Eve did. Animals were important in Eden, when the earth was perfect. So they'll probably be important on the New Earth, where everything will once again be perfect.

Remember Elijah? He was taken up to Heaven in a chariot pulled by horses (2 Kings 2:11). We're told there are horses in Heaven (Revelation 6:2-8). In fact, there are enough horses for all who are in the vast armies of Heaven to ride (Revelation 19:14). There are also armies of angels currently riding horses on Earth, even though they're invisible to us (2 Kings 6:17).

No other animals are mentioned in Revelation, probably because they don't play a role in Christ's second coming. (An army that comes to save God's people rides horses, not squirrels, anteaters, or guinea pigs.) But isn't it likely that since there are so many horses in Heaven, there are all kinds of other animals too? Why wouldn't there be? Why would we expect horses to be the only animals in Heaven?

Some people think the horses in the present Heaven are just a picture from Earth of something else totally different. However, even those people have to admit that a New Earth wouldn't be complete without animals. Since we know resurrected people in real bodies will live there on real ground, with real trees and mountains and rivers, there's no reason why there won't be real animals, too. In a passage speaking of the New Earth, God says animals—wolf, lamb, and lion among them—will lie down in peace together (Isaiah 65:25). While some people think this refers only to a temporary kingdom that will last a thousand years, I think it refers also to the eternal New Earth.

Jesus proclaims from his throne on New Earth: "I am making all things new" (Revelation 21:5, ESV). Jesus is talking about making old things new, rather than just making new things (not that he couldn't make new things). He seems to be saying, "I'll take all I made the first time, including people, nature, animals, and the earth itself, and bring it back in a way that's new, fresh, and unable to be destroyed." I believe this suggests that God may remake certain animals that lived on the old Earth. — Randy Alcorn and Linda Washington, *Heaven for Kids* (Carol Stream, IL: Tyndale, 2006).

## 18. Do you think there will be laughter in Heaven?

Who said, "If you're not allowed to laugh in heaven, I don't want to go there"? (Hint: It wasn't Mark Twain.) The answer is, Martin Luther. In Heaven, I believe our joy will often erupt in laughter. When laughter is prompted by what's appropriate, God always takes pleasure in it. I think Christ will laugh with us, and his wit and fun-loving nature will be our greatest sources of endless laughter.

Where did humor originate? Not with people, angels, or Satan. God created all good things, including good humor. If God didn't have a sense of humor, human beings, as his image-bearers, wouldn't either. Of course, if God didn't have a sense of humor, we probably also wouldn't have aardvarks, baboons, platypuses, and giraffes. You have to smile when you picture one of these, don't you?

There's nothing like the laughter of dear friends. The Bible often portrays us around the dinner table in God's coming Kingdom. What sound do you hear when friends gather to eat and talk? The sound of laughter.

My wife, Nanci, loves football. She opens our home to family and friends for Monday night football. Right now there are five toddlers in the group, and they keep us laughing. If you came to our house on Monday nights, you'd hear cheers and groans for the football teams, but the dominant sound in the room, week after week, is laughter. There are stories from family and work, and heart-to-heart talks, and pausing to pray—all surrounded by laughter. God made us to laugh and to love to laugh.

The new universe will ring with laughter. Am I just speculating about this? No. I can point to Scripture worth memorizing. Jesus said, "Blessed are you who hunger now, for you will be satisfied. Blessed are you who weep now, for you will laugh" (Luke 6:21). You will laugh.

Where will we be satisfied? In Heaven. Where will we laugh?

In Heaven. Can we be certain of that? Yes, because Jesus tells us precisely where this promise will be fulfilled: "Rejoice in that day and leap for joy, because great is your reward in heaven" (Luke 6:23).

Just as Jesus promises satisfaction as a reward in Heaven, he also promises laughter as a reward. Anticipating the laughter to come, Jesus says we should "leap for joy" now. Can you imagine someone leaping for joy in utter silence, without laughter? Take any group of rejoicing people, and what do you hear? Laughter. There may be hugging, backslapping, playful wrestling, singing, and storytelling. But always there is laughter. It is God's gift to humanity.

Surely laughter will not contract, but expand in the final resurrection.

The reward of those who mourn now will be laughter later. Passages such as Luke 6 gave the early Christians strength to endure persecution in "an understanding of heaven as the compensation for lost earthly privileges." In early Christian Greek tradition, Easter Monday was a "day of joy and laughter," called Bright Monday. Only the followers of Christ can laugh in the face of persecution and death because they know that their present trouble isn't all there is. They know that someday they will laugh.

By God's grace, we can laugh right now, even under death's shadow. Jesus doesn't say, "If you weep, soon things on Earth will take a better turn, and then you'll laugh." Things won't always take a better turn on an Earth under the Curse. Sickness, loss, grief, and death will find us. Just as our reward will come in Heaven, laughter (itself one of our rewards) will come in Heaven, compensating for our present sorrow. God won't only wipe away all our tears, he'll fill our hearts with joy and our mouths with laughter. — Randy Alcorn, *50 Days of Heaven: Reflections That Bring Eternity to Light* (Carol Stream, IL: Tyndale, 2006).

## 19. Do you think it would do us good to think more about Heaven than we do?

Over the years, a number of people have told me, "We shouldn't think about Heaven. We should just think about Jesus."

This viewpoint sounds spiritual, doesn't it? But it is based on wrong assumptions, and it is clearly contradicted by Scripture.

Colossians 3:1-2 is a direct command to set our hearts and minds on Heaven. We set our minds on Heaven because we love Jesus Christ, and Heaven is where he now resides. To long for Heaven is to long for Christ. To long for Christ is to long for Heaven, for that is where we will be with him. That's why God's people are "longing for a better country" (Hebrews 11:16).

In Colossians 3:1, the Greek word translated "set your hearts on" is zeteo, which "denotes man's general philosophical search or quest." The same word is used in the Gospels to describe how "the Son of Man came to seek and to save what was lost" (Luke 19:10, emphasis added). Zeteo is also used to describe how a shepherd looks for his lost sheep (Matthew 18:12), a woman searches for a lost coin (Luke 15:8), and a merchant searches for fine pearls (Matthew 13:45). It is a diligent, active, single-minded pursuit. Thus, we can understand Paul's admonition in Colossians 3:1 as follows: "Diligently, actively, single-mindedly pursue the things above"—in a word, Heaven.

The verb zeteo is in the present tense, suggesting an ongoing process. "Keep seeking Heaven." Don't just have a conversation, read a book, or listen to a sermon and feel as if you've fulfilled the command. If you're going to spend the next lifetime living in Heaven, why not spend this lifetime seeking Heaven so you can eagerly anticipate and prepare for it?

The command, and its restatement, implies there is nothing automatic about setting our minds on Heaven. In fact, most commands assume a resistance to obeying them, which sets up the necessity for the command. We are told to avoid sexual immorality because it is our tendency. We are not told to avoid jumping off buildings because normally we don't battle such a temptation. Every day, the command to think about Heaven is under attack in a hundred different ways. Everything militates against thinking about Heaven. Our minds are set so resolutely on Earth that we are unaccustomed to heavenly thinking. So we must work at it.

What have you been doing daily to set your mind on things above, to seek Heaven? What should you do differently?

Perhaps you're afraid of becoming "so heavenly minded that you're of no earthly good." Relax—you have nothing to worry about! On the contrary, many of us are so earthly minded we are of no heavenly or earthly good. As C. S. Lewis observed,

> If you read history you will find that the Christians who did most for the present world were just those who thought most of the next. The Apostles themselves, who set on foot the conversion of the Roman Empire, the great men who built up the Middle Ages, the English Evangelicals who abolished the Slave Trade, all left their mark on Earth, precisely because their minds were occupied with Heaven. It is since Christians have largely ceased to think of the other world that they have become so ineffective in this. Aim at Heaven and you will get earth "thrown in": aim at earth and you will get neither.

We need a generation of heavenly minded people who see human beings and the earth itself not simply as they are, but as God intends them to be. Such people will pass on a heritage to their children far more valuable than any inheritance. — Randy Alcorn, *50 Days of Heaven: Reflections That Bring Eternity to Light* (Carol Stream, IL: Tyndale, 2006).

## 20. How does hope of Heaven affect our life now?

These heavenly citizens are an overcoming people (vv. 7-8). "He that overcometh" is a key phrase in this book (Rev. 2:7, 11, 17, 26; 3:5, 12, 21; note also 12:11). As John pointed out in his first epistle, all true believers are overcomers (1 John 5:4-5), so this promise is not just for the "spiritually elite." Because we are the children of God, we shall inherit all things.

After the great Chicago fire of 1871, evangelist Dwight L. Moody went back to survey the ruins of his house. A friend came by and said to Moody, "I hear you lost everything."

"Well," said Moody, "you understood wrong. I have a good deal more left than I lost."

"What do you mean?" the inquisitive friend asked. "I didn't know you were that rich."

Moody then opened his Bible and read to him Revelation 21:7—"He that overcometh shall inherit all things, and I will be his God." — *The Bible Exposition Commentary – New Testament, Volume 2.*

## 21. What do you want to recall from today's discussion?

## 22. How can we support one another in prayer this week?

CPSIA information can be obtained
at www.ICGtesting.com
Printed in the USA
BVHW011342300920
590001BV00015B/429

9 781508 767800